Pre-Inter

D0549331

Just

Reading and Writing

For class or self-study

Ana Acavedo
Carol Lethaby
Jeremy Harmer

with Cheryl Pelteret

Marshall Cavendish
Education

© 2007 Marshall Cavendish Education

First published 2007 by Marshall Cavendish Education
Marshall Cavendish is a member of the Times Publishing Group

ISBN: (10 digit) 0 462 00774 X
      (13 digit) 978 04620 0774 8

Marshall Cavendish Education
119 Wardour Street
London W1F 0UW

Designed by Hart McLeod, Cambridge
Illustrations by Jo Taylor, Yane Christiansen, Francis Fung, Rory Walker,
Valeryia Steadman, Tim Oliver

Printed and bound by Times Offset (M) Sdn Bhd

Contents

Introduction

For the student

Welcome to *Just Reading and Writing*. You can use this book with other students and a teacher, or you can work alone with it. It will help you improve your reading and writing skills.

There are sixteen units in this book. We have chosen topics which we hope you will find interesting. You will find articles and stories, and emails and other text-types too.

This book has many practice exercises to help you with reading and writing. When you see this symbol (⬤━) you can find answers in the answer key at the back of the book. You can check your answers there.

We hope that you enjoy using this book and that it will help you progress in English.

For the teacher

This book is part of a series designed to supplement any course book you may be using. Each book in the series specialises in either language skills or aspects of the English language itself. It is designed to be used either in class or by students working on their own.

Just Reading and Writing consists of 16 units, containing a variety of reading texts on subjects such as stress, memory, crocodile hunters, emails from abroad, hobbies and intelligence. These are designed to give students experience of reading and writing in different styles of English. There are also exercises which the student will be able to use even if a teacher is unavailable for explanations or guidance. There is a comprehensive answer key, and where free writing is required an 'example answer' is usually given.

How you use the material in class is up to you, of course. Our aim has been to provide stimulating texts and tasks which can lead to any number of different activities once the exercises in this book have been completed.

We hope you find this book useful and that you will also try the other books in the series; *Just Vocabulary*, *Just Grammar* and *Just Listening and Speaking*.

•••A Reading: Holiday postcards

1 Read the postcards quickly and match them with the countries.

a South Africa ☐
b Australia ☐
c The USA ☐
d Canada ☐

2 Find the answers to these questions.

a What is one of the languages people speak in Montreal? ....

b Who is not having a good time? ....

c Who did not enjoy their journey? ....

d Which city is at the foot of a mountain?

....

e Where are there no big towns? ....

f Which city will Jessy go to next? ....

g Whose family comes from the place she is visiting? ....

3 Read the postcards again. Write T (true) or F (False) in the boxes.

a You can swim in Cape Town. ☐
b Wyoming is a big city. ☐
c Jerry likes big cities. ☐
d The Great Barrier Reef is an ocean. ☐
e The Saint Lawrence River is in Montreal. ☐
f Table Mountain is near Sydney. ☐

1

Dear Mum and Dad,
The flight was tiring and boring but here we are at last! The Great Barrier Reef is huge – more than 2000 kilometres long! It's simply amazing. You can see lots of different (beautiful) fish, they say. We are taking the train to Sydney on Tuesday. We will write again from there.
Love ya Jessy

2

Hi everyone!
Montreal is beautiful! We went on a great city tour. We also took a boat ride on the Saint Lawrence River, but it's nicer to just sit at a street café and watch the world go by. Dad's disappointed because nobody can understand his French!
Take care!
Mum and Dad

3

Hi!
Cape Town is at the foot of Table Mountain. It's beautiful, modern and exciting. The beaches are great, and the nightlife is better! I am really excited because my dad was born here! Everyone is very friendly and we have met lots of interesting people. I'm thinking of you all back home, cold and bored!
XXXX
Tricia

4

Hi guys!
We're staying on a ranch in Wyoming. There is absolutely nothing around here – it's the middle of NOWHERE! Every morning we get up really early and we go for a ride on the horses. Then it's breakfast and more riding – not my idea of fun! So today I walked to this little town to bu this postcard. Next week we go to San Francisc I can't wait. I like cities better than the count
Jerry

4 Find words in the postcards that mean the opposite of:

a boring ....

b old-fashioned ....

c similar ....

d tiny ....

e worse ....

· ·

5 Rewrite the <u>underlined</u> phrases, using one of the phrases below.

a It's <u>in the middle of nowhere</u>! ....

b Cape Town is <u>at the foot</u> of Table Mountain. ....

c It's nicer to sit at a street café and <u>watch the world go by</u>. ....

d Then it's breakfast and more riding – not <u>my idea of fun</u>! ....

e I <u>can't wait</u>. ....

f The <u>nightlife</u> is better. ....

> 1 am excited
> 2 at the bottom
> 3 look at people and things
> 4 on its own, in an empty space
> 5 what I enjoy
> 6 discos, pubs, clubs, etc.

· ·

6 Now use the <u>underlined</u> phrases to complete this conversation.

A: Have you heard my news? We're going to Australia next summer!
I (**a**) .... – it's been my dream
for such a long time.

B: Yes, it's a great place. I love Sydney. People always think of the
great beaches there, but the (**b**) ....
is fantastic, too.

A: Did you go to the outback?

B: Yes, we went on a camping trip. It was really boring, stuck
(**c**) .... with no shops or other
people. Some people love the quiet life, but it's certainly not
(**d**) ....

A: Yes, I know what you mean. I much prefer to lie on a beach or sit
in cafés and just (**e**) ....

B: Well, you must visit The Rocks, then. It's an area full of cafés,
markets, shops and bars, (**f**) .... of
Sydney Harbour Bridge. If you like watching people, this is the
place to go!

B Writing: Postcards

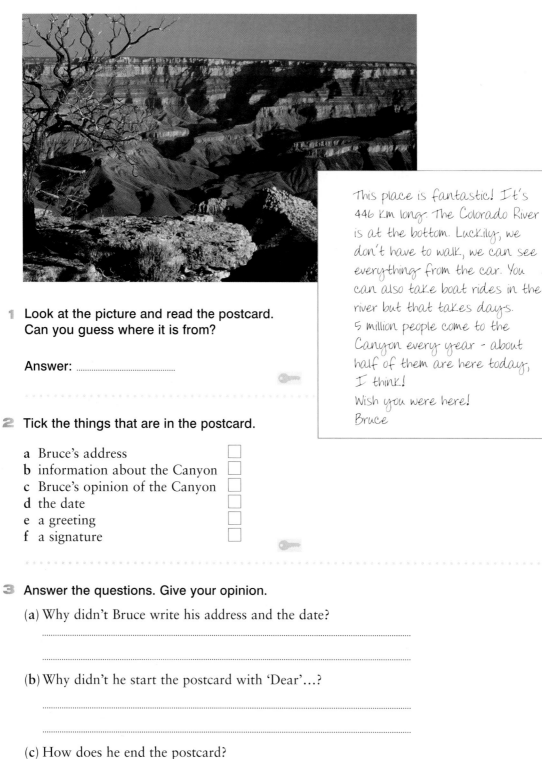

This place is fantastic! It's 446 km long. The Colorado River is at the bottom. Luckily, we don't have to walk, we can see everything from the car. You can also take boat rides in the river but that takes days.
5 million people come to the Canyon every year - about half of them are here today, I think!
Wish you were here!
Bruce

1 Look at the picture and read the postcard. Can you guess where it is from?

Answer: ....

2 Tick the things that are in the postcard.

a Bruce's address ☐
b information about the Canyon ☐
c Bruce's opinion of the Canyon ☐
d the date ☐
e a greeting ☐
f a signature ☐

3 Answer the questions. Give your opinion.

(a) Why didn't Bruce write his address and the date?

....

....

(b) Why didn't he start the postcard with 'Dear'...?

....

....

(c) How does he end the postcard?

....

....

(d) Why? ....

4 Use the notes to write a postcard to your friend,
   Jan, about the Taj Mahal, in India.

The Taj Mahal

* beautiful building in the city of
  Agra, India
* built by Shah Jahan in 1631,
  when his second wife died
* made entirely of marble and
  jewels brought from all over India
* amazing: took 22 years to
  complete, by 20,000 workers,
  and 1,000 elephants!

Jan Brookes

5 Now use the checklist and read your postcard again.

	Yes	No
Have you written 'Dear Jan'?		
Have you written your address?		
Have you written the date?		
Have you written some facts?		
Have you written some opinions (adjectives)?		
Have you used postcard language (e.g. 'wish you were here')?		

•••A Reading: Stress

1 Choose a phrase from the box to complete each sentence. Put the verb in the right tense.

to have bad dreams	to feel angry
to have headaches	to forget things
to sweat a lot	to feel nervous

a He _is having a bad dream._

b She ....

c He ....

d She often

....

e He is feeling hot and

....

f She ....

2 Read these dictionary definitions. Look quickly at the text. Which meaning (1 or 2) is the text about?

....

stress /stres/ **n 1** the feeling of being worried because of problems in your life. **2** special force we put onto a word or part of a word.

3 Before you read the text closely, guess whether these statements are true or false. Write T or F in the boxes.

a Most people find changes stressful. ☐
b Stress can sometimes help you to do well. ☐
c You shouldn't eat sugary snacks when you are feeling stressed. ☐
d Drinking coffee can help you feel less stressed. ☐
e You shouldn't do exercise when you are stressed. ☐

4 Read the text. As you read, think about the questions in the blue boxes. What are your answers?

a ....

Do you ever feel that you don't know what to do because there are too many things in your life? Then you probably feel stress. Things that cause stress are called 'stressors'. One important stressor is change. For example, going to a new school or starting a new job can give you stress. Other common stressors are taking a test or being ill.

> Think about changes in your life. Did they cause you stress?

b ....

But some stress can be good. For example, before a race most athletes feel nervous. This stress helps them get ready.

> Can you think of a time when stress helped you get ready?

What makes stress good or bad? Let's look at an example: Jack has a new job in another city. He and his wife are very excited. But their children are sad to leave their family and friends. The move to another city is a good stressor for the parents but a bad one for the children. The parents and the children have different feelings about the situation.

> What is a good stressor for you? What is a bad one?

c ....

When you are feeling stressed, these tips can help you:
- Eat lots of fruit and vegetables and meat and fish without fat. Salad is good too. Don't eat any snacks, like crisps, and don't drink any caffeine.
- Don't eat too much sugar – put the chocolate and cakes away.
- Do exercise every day. Laugh! Make time for fun.
- Talk about your problems.

> What do you do when you are stressed? Do you use any of the tips?

5 Write the paragraph headings in the right places in the text, a, b or c.

How to deal with stress

What is stress?

Different kinds of stress

6 Read the text again. Write:

a a definition of stress ....

b a definition of 'stressor' ....

c an important stressor ....

d things that can make stress good or bad ....

e some things that can make you feel better ....

f food that is bad for you when you are stressed ....

●●●B Writing: *because, but, so*

1   **Read the problems from students of English. In a – d write
the word that helps you answer the questions.**

'I get stressed when
I read in English
because there are
many words I don't
know.'
Boris, Moscow, Russia

'Sometimes I can't do
the grammar exercises,
so I get stressed.'
Amel, Cairo, Egypt

'I like to speak in
English, but I worry
about my
pronunciation.'
Feçir, Ankara, Turkey

'I want to learn lots of
words, but I don't
know how.'
Koji, Nagoya, Japan

a   Boris gets stressed – what is the reason? ....Because.......................................

b   Amel can't do the grammar exercises – what is the result of this? ....

c   Feçir likes to speak English – what is the problem? ....

d   Koji wants to learn new words – what is the problem? ....

2   **Complete the sentences with *because*, *but* or *so*.**

a   There are many words I don't know, ... I can use a dictionary.

b   I write down new words, ... I can look at them again and remember them.

c   I want to learn English .... it is important for many jobs.

d   English is sometimes difficult, ... I like it.

e   I like having a workbook, ... it has a lot of exercises.

f   Sometimes I don't understand, ... I can ask my teacher for help.

3 Is learning English stressful? Read the ideas on these two pages about learning English. Use the ideas to complete the leaflet. Use *because, but* and *so* where necessary.

Learning English can help you get a better job.

I always keep a small notebook with me. I use it to look up words or write down things.

I think repeating things over and over helps me to remember them.

It's nice to be able to understand films and songs in English.

Take a deep breath and relax. When you are relaxed, you learn more.

English is important. It's the most widely spoken international language.

Take the stress out of learning English!

Why is learning English a good idea?

⟹

⟹

⟹

Things about English that can be stressful.

⟹

⟹

⟹

Things you can do to help yourself.

⟹

⟹

⟹

•••A Reading: Do the media decide?

1 Look at the photos and the title of the article. What do you think the article will be about? Circle a, b or c.

a the influence of the media on people's lives

b a girl who wants to be a model

c popular magazines

Are the media a bad influence?

Kirsty is fifteen years old. She likes doing what every other girl her age enjoys. She goes to school, she watches TV and goes shopping with her friends. But Kirsty has an ambition: she wants to be a model. Every week, she saves her pocket money to buy magazines. She studies the photos of famous models. They are her role models. Kirsty's mother, Stella, is not happy. 'It's OK to have ambitions,' she says. 'But in Kirsty's case it's becoming an obsession. She thinks about it all the time.' According to Stella, Kirsty does not have a healthy diet and she exercises more than normal because she wants to be thin. She worries that Kirsty is developing an eating disorder. 'The media are responsible for this situation,' her mum says. 'All the teen magazines and teen programmes on TV tell children that the only important thing is how you look – your appearance. They say, "You want to be happy? Then be thin!"'

Are the media really responsible for situations like Kirsty's? Kirsty's big sister Donna, 18, disagrees. 'I buy lots of magazines but I don't want to be like the people in them,' says Donna. 'Magazines show you all kinds of people, not just celebrities. They give information and have nice pictures. That's why I like them.'

So, who is right? Do the media decide how we look and how we live? Are we all becoming obsessed with celebrities and their lifestyles?

2 **Answer the following questions:**

Why ...

a does Kirsty buy magazines? ....

b does Donna like magazines? ....

How ...

c does Kirsty keep thin? ....

d does Stella feel about Kirsty? ....

What ...

e does Stella think about the media? ....

f does she think about having ambitions? ....

- -

3 **Find words in blue in the text which mean:**

a you want to copy these people because you think they are fantastic ....

b parents give their children this money to spend ....

c something you can't stop thinking about – all the time! ....

d you have this when you really want to do well ....

e the power to change what people think or do ....

f a medical problem – you don't eat normally ....

g you are this when you are the cause of something or the reason for something ....

- -

4 **Now use the words in blue to complete these sentences.**

a After years of dieting, she developed an .... which is making her very ill.

b I didn't get any .... when I was a teenager – I had to get a Saturday job.

c She goes to the gym twice a day – it's become an .... for her to get fit.

d Some people say that TV advertisements are .... for children's love of junk food.

e These days the .... for lots of young people are celebrities, or famous sports personalities.

f When I was younger, it was my .... to become a pop star.

g Even though he is an adult now, his parents still have a lot of .... on the way he thinks.

●●●B Writing: Survey report

1 Read the survey report and answer the questions.

TELEVISION: SURVEY REPORT

Sample: 240 people between the ages of 18 and 35 were interviewed.

1 Hours spent watching television
70% of people asked watch 4-6 hours
25% watch 2-4 hours
5% watch less than two hours

2 Preferences
45% of people asked prefer sitcoms to any other programme
35% prefer soap operas
15% prefer documentaries
5% prefer news programmes

3 Reasons for watching TV
75% of people asked watch for entertainment
18% watch for information
7% watch to learn new things (for educational purposes)

Conclusion: Most people watch between 4-6 hours every day. Sitcoms are the most popular programme in this age group. Most people watch television for entertainment. Few of the people in this age group are interested in the news.

a How many people answered questions? ....

b How old were they? ....

c How many people watch TV for more than four hours a day? ....

d What kind of programme do most people watch? ....

e Are there any people who watch TV to learn new things? ....

2 Look at the diagram. Write T (true) or F (false) in the boxes.

a Most people like sitcoms. ☐

b A lot of people like the news. ☐

c More people like documentaries than sitcoms. ☐

d More people like documentaries than the news. ☐

e On average, everyone watches TV about two hours a week. ☐

f Not many people like soap operas. ☐

7 of us like news. We watch TV for 2 hours a day.

3 of us like sitcoms. We watch TV for 2 hours a day.

8 of us like soap operas. We watch TV for 3 hours a day.

5 of us like documentaries. We watch TV for 3 hours a day.

3 Now write the correct answers where necessary.

....

....

....

4 Complete these sentences about the survey in exercise 1. Use the words in the box.

(a) .... people enjoy sitcoms than any other programme. (b) .... of people watch soap operas, too. According to the survey, (c) .... people younger than 35 don't watch the news. The (d) .... number of hours people watch TV every day, is five. (e) .... people, it seems, watch TV to find out new things.

not many	a lot
most	more
average	

5 Now look at this graph. Which question in the survey is being shown? Write 1, 2 or 3 in the box.

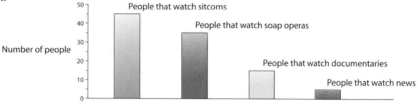

Number of people

50
40
30
20
10
0

People that watch sitcoms
People that watch soap operas
People that watch documentaries
People that watch news

6 Look at the results of this survey.

How many people read popular magazines?

We asked 100 people between the ages of 16 and 30.

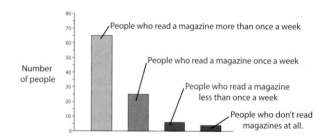

Number of people

80
70
60
50
40
30
20
10
0

People who read a magazine more than once a week
People who read a magazine once a week
People who read a magazine less than once a week
People who don't read magazines at all.

Number of people	More than once a week	Once a week	Less than once a week	Not at all

7 Now write a short report about the results of the survey. Use the model in exercise 1 to help you.

...A Reading: Crocodile hunter

1 Read the text quickly and find out:

a the name of the crocodile hunter ....

b his wife's name and her occupation ....

c where their Reptile and Fauna Park is ....

d what other animals the couple catch . ...

The crocodile hunter

When he was six, Steve Irwin got his first pet animal. It was a very large snake. This was the start of his hobby and by the age of twelve he was helping his father catch crocodiles, or 'jump crocs' as he calls it.

When someone with a pet snake at six years old grows up, what does he do? He becomes a reptile expert, a herpetologist, or 'herp' for short. And Steve Irwin became Australia's most famous crocodile hunter. Now Steve and his wife Terri, an American lion tamer, run a wildlife park in Queensland, Australia.

Although Steve is called a 'crocodile hunter', he doesn't kill the animals; instead, he moves 'problem' crocodiles to safe environments. These rogue crocodiles live in popular fishing and swimming areas where tourists like to go and so, of course, they are a danger to people. Steve can move crocs up to eight feet long (2.44 metres) with his bare hands.

But the Irwins don't just catch crocodiles. They also catch dangerous snakes and 'milk', or collect, their venom to make anti-toxin (that's medicine to help people with snake bites). And how does Steve catch snakes? With his bare hands of course!

The Irwins first became famous through their popular television series, 'The Crocodile Hunter'. 'Saltwater crocodiles are the largest reptiles in the world,' says Steve. 'People are scared of them and shoot them. Through our programme, people can learn about these animals and learn to respect them.'

So, are you interested in reptiles? Are you looking for an exciting, unusual occupation? Then maybe you too can become a herpetologist, like Steve. But please don't try his tricks at home!

2 Read the text again and answer the questions.

What ...

a is a herpetologist? ....

b does Steve Irwin do with the crocodiles he catches? ....

c was Terri's previous occupation? ....

Why ...

d did Steve become a crocodile hunter? ....

e does he catch snakes? ....

f does Steve think their programme is important? ....

g do people shoot crocodiles? ....

When ...

h did Steve first become interested in reptiles? ....

i did the Irwins first become famous? ....

How ....

j does Steve catch snakes? ....

3 Find these words and phrases in the text and match them with their definitions on the right.

a 'jump crocs'	**1** in the sea
b 'milk' (a snake's venom)	**2** poison
c herpetologist	**3** without any instruments
d anti-toxin	**4** catch crocodiles
e rogue (crocodiles)	**5** someone who knows all about reptiles
f venom	**6** living away from the rest of the group
g with his bare hands	**7** medicine to help fight poison
h saltwater	**8** obtain

a .... b ....

c .... d ....

e .... f ....

g .... h ....

4 Complete the word grid with words from the text. The word in the shaded column means 'job'.

a the opposite of safe

b to admire and treat politely

c the opposite of boring

d something special, not ordinary

e well liked by many people

f naked

g snakes, crocodiles, lizards

h someone who visits a place

i a big, wild cat

j the area where something lives

a: d a n g e r o u s
b
c
d
e
f
g
h
i
j

B Writing: Small ads

1 Read the ads. Who is offering a job? Who is looking for a job?

Advertisement a ....
Advertisement b ....

. . . .

2 Put the following information in the same sequence as in the advertisements on the right. Write 1 – 5 in the boxes.

Ad a

a the name of the person looking for a job ☐

b the person's skills ☐

c a contact number ☐

d extra, important information about the person ☐

e what the person is looking for ☐

Ad b

a the name of the company ☐

b what the company is looking for ☐

c what the company offers ☐

d what the company needs ☐

e a contact number ☐

---

a

Wanted

I am a student looking for temporary office work.
I can speak English and I have good computer skills.
I have no experience **but** I am a fast learner.

Please ring Carrie on 3759670, evenings.

---

b

WANTED

We are looking for temporary staff in our offices. We require:
Good presentation
Good English
Good computing skills
We offer:
A good salary
Free sports club
Free lunches at the company's restaurant
Call 75953795 **NOW!**
Kimber and Kimber Associates

3 Read the picture story.

4 Now use the information in exercise 3 to complete the small ad.

WANTED

Popular magazine publishing company
(Music Scene, Fashion World, etc.)
needs an .... in our offices.
Hours would suit .... :
(....)
Requirements: ....

....

We offer: ....

....

Call .... , on ....

●●●A Reading: The station

1 What kind of story does the extract come from? Tick the correct box.

a a romance/love story ☐

b a science fiction story ☐

c a thriller/spy story ☐

d a horror story ☐

When he came into the station, Ferdy looked down at all the people below him. Ah yes. There she was. Amelie. The beautiful Amelie, with her long, black hair and her incredible blue, blue eyes. She was waiting for him.

Ferdy's eyes scanned the scene in front of him, and then he looked up. Above him two men were working on the roof. He could see them through the glass. What were they doing there? Perhaps they were cleaning the glass. But perhaps they weren't.

He tried to act normally. He got onto the escalator and went down towards the platforms just like any other normal person. But that was the problem. He wasn't normal. He was different from other people.

Opposite him was the entrance to the platform – her platform. Amelie was standing under the number 7. Perhaps everything was OK.

But then he saw two young women in yellow hard hats. They were standing by the coffee stall. He noticed something. They weren't talking or drinking coffee. They were watching everyone in the station, but when he looked at them, they looked away.

Suddenly he heard a noise. Someone inside the ticket office was shouting into a mobile phone. He turned his head. It was an old man, and next to him was a woman. His wife?

Nothing to worry about. But then the old man saw him. He stopped shouting. He took his mobile phone from his ear. He just stared.

Platform 7 was in front of him now. Amelie saw him. She smiled.

Suddenly a woman walked between him and Amelie. She didn't look happy. Then he knew. He was in danger.

Ferdy looked behind him. There was no one. He turned round and ran back up the escalator and into the street. He heard Amelie call his name.

There were three men standing outside and they were waiting for him.

2 Look at the picture and read the text again. There are four mistakes in the picture. What are they?

Mistake 1	
2	
3	
4	

3 Read the text again and circle the best answer, 1, 2 or 3.

a Amelie was at the station because …
   1 she was going to catch a train.
   2 she was meeting Ferdy.
   3 she was in danger.

b It was difficult for Ferdy to act normally, because …
   1 people were looking at him.
   2 he was on an escalator.
   3 he wasn't like everyone else.

c The two women were standing by the coffee stall because …
   1 they were watching everyone.
   2 they were drinking coffee.
   3 they were talking on mobile phones.

d When the old man saw Ferdy, he …
   1 began talking on his mobile phone.
   2 began talking to his wife.
   3 stopped and stared.

e Ferdy realized he was in danger when …
   1 he saw three men waiting for him outside.
   2 he heard Amelie call his name.
   3 he saw a woman who looked unhappy.

4 Write the words in blue from the text in the blanks. The first one is done for you.

a looked from side to side very quickly to get a general view ....*scanned*........................

b moving stairs ....

c the top part of the building ....

d the same as other people – not different ....

e be unhappy / anxious about something and think about it a lot ....

f looked at someone for a long time – without moving your head ....

g turned quickly and looked at something different ....

h very, very beautiful, fantastic ....

5 Now use the words in blue to complete these sentences.

a He .... at the beautiful painting for a long time.

b You'll have to walk up the stairs, because the .... is broken.

c The fireworks display was the most .... one I have ever seen.

d It's .... to feel nervous before an exam.

e She .... shyly when I tried to make eye contact.

f Don't .... driving me home later, I'll take a taxi.

g There was such a storm last night, it nearly blew the .... off.

h I .... the list of exam results, hoping to see my name.

B Writing: Direction emails

1 Match the directions with the diagrams.

a Take the first left. ☐

b Take the second right. ☐

c It's on the right. ☐

d Turn left. ☐

e Go along … ☐

f Turn right. ☐

g It's on the left. ☐

h It's on the corner. ☐

....

2 Use some of the directions above, and put them in the correct order to describe the route on the map.

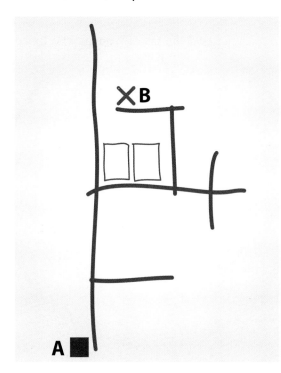

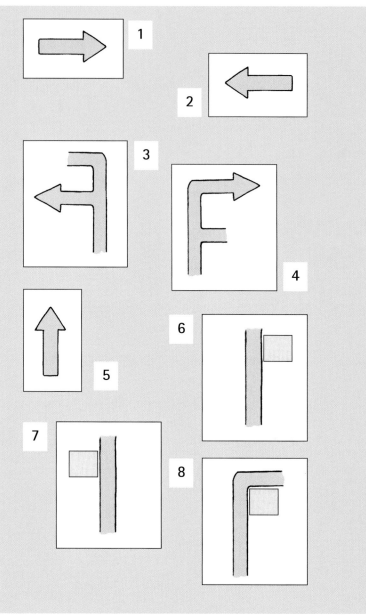

3 Read the email and choose the correct map.

The correct map is ....

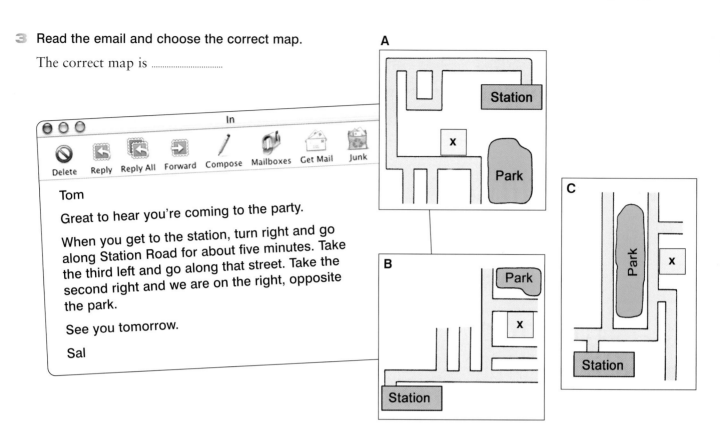

Tom

Great to hear you're coming to the party.

When you get to the station, turn right and go along Station Road for about five minutes. Take the third left and go along that street. Take the second right and we are on the right, opposite the park.

See you tomorrow.

Sal

4 Now complete the email for one of the other two maps. Which map is it?

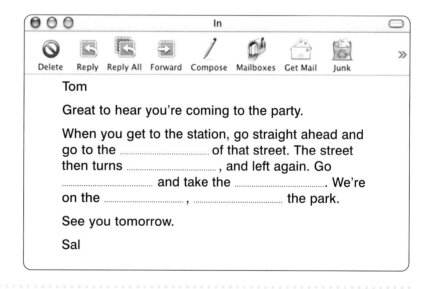

Tom

Great to hear you're coming to the party.

When you get to the station, go straight ahead and go to the .... of that street. The street then turns ...., and left again. Go .... and take the .... We're on the ...., ... the park.

See you tomorrow.

Sal

5 Write directions for the other map in exercise 3. Use language from the email.

....

....

....

....

....

●●●A Reading: Short-term and long-term memory

1 Read the text and find out:

a why we often forget people's names.

....

b what kind of things bring back memories from long ago.

....

c how we manage to remember important facts in a test.

....

d why we don't usually forget things we have learned to do, like riding a bike.

....

I want to know about... MEMORY

Dr Gita Patel, a memory expert, answers your questions.

Q: I met a guy at a party. We met again a few days later and I couldn't remember his name! I felt bad. What's wrong with my memory?

A: We all forget things. We throw away information that we don't need any more. You put the man's name in your *short-term memory*. That's the bit of your brain that keeps things you don't need to remember for very long – like a telephone number you only use once. You forgot the man's name because it wasn't very important to you.

Q: What is long-term memory?

A: *Long-term memory* is where we keep information we need to remember for a long time. It is like a filing cabinet with different drawers. One drawer contains memories of things that happened to you a long time ago, like your first day at school or a summer holiday. This is your *episodic* memory. It stores the episodes that make up your life. You don't think about these things all the time. But then something, like a smell or a song brings that memory back and suddenly you remember everything about it. Another drawer is your *semantic* memory. In this drawer the brain keeps information like important historical dates and facts about your country. Your brain only opens this drawer when you need to use the information, for example in a test.

Q: People say you never forget how to do things like riding a bicycle. Is this true?

A: Yes. This is called *procedural* memory because it stores procedures, or the way to do things. It helps you to remember skills you learned in your life, things like how to ride a bike or how to use a mobile phone. These memories stay in the brain all your life.

2 Write T (true) or F (false) in the boxes.

a Everybody forgets things. ☐

b We forget information that we don't need any more. ☐

c The writer of the first question really wanted to remember the name of the man she met. ☐

d Dates (e.g. from history) are stored in the same place as events in your life. ☐

e Semantic memory can be useful in exams. ☐

f A smell can bring back memories. ☐

g Procedural memory allows you to remember telephone numbers. ☐

3 Write the notes in the correct places in the chart to help you remember the meanings of the words.

Information about how to do things
Information that is no longer necessary to keep
Information that needs to be stored for a long time
Important facts or dates
Things that happened a long time ago

	NOTES
Short-term memory	
Long-term memory	
Episodic memory	
Procedural memory	
Semantic memory	

4 Find words from the text in blue which mean:

a a piece of furniture to keep files in (noun)

....

b not right (adjective)

....

c a particular event in your life (noun) ....

d the ability to remember things in the past (noun)

....

e particular events or experiences you remember from the past (noun)

....

f to put or keep in a special place (verb) ....

g to bring back a memory (verb) ....

•••B Writing: Life story website

1   Read the message. What do Kensuke and Lisa want? Why?

....   🔑

Home | Contact us | Links | Help & Information

Remember us?

We're Kensuke Sato (aka Cat) and Lisa
García (aka Panther). Kensuke and I
both went to The International School
in Los Angeles. We are original
members of the band The Zoo. After
school, Kensuke went back to Japan
and I went back to Mexico and life went
on. Last year Kensuke and I were
reunited through 'Together Again'.
We are getting married next summer!
We want to get the band together again
to play at our wedding. Did you use to
play in The Zoo? Do you want to re-live
happy memories? Bear, Rhino and Fox,
where are you? Get in touch to share
all the old stories!

2   Look at the website again. Tick the items that are included.

a names ☐

b addresses ☐

c name of school ☐

d personal information about the past ☐

e details about the people's careers ☐

f the reason why they want to find their friends ☐   🔑

3 Now read this person's personal details and complete his life story website.

> **Name**: Riccardo Bruni (aka Bear)
> **School**: International School Los Angeles
> **Activities at school**: played in band called The Zoo
> **After school**: went to New York – got job teaching kids guitar. Then, went back to Italy – got job as music teacher in school – met Anna – got married last year! Now – a baby, Marco.

Home | Contact us | Links | Help & Information

Hello Cat and Panther!

Remember me? I'm ....
.... I was at
.... too, and we
played in ....
.... I played the ....
and the piano. Do you know I became a music teacher?
After school, ...
.... My first job was ....
.... It was OK, but
the money was terrible! Then I ....
.... and started
working as .... at
.... There I
.... and she's now
my wife! We ....
last year. Now we've got ....
.... I hope you meet them both
soon, when we come and play at your wedding!
Please, Rhino and Fox, tell us where you are!

4 Use the personal details of this person, and write her life story website.

> **Name:** Jiao Tsim (aka Fox)
> **School:** International School Los Angeles
> **Activities at school:** singer in band called The Zoo
> **After school:** went back to China – studied English at Beijing University – wrote book of children's stories last year – now working on another book. Not married yet – too busy!

•••A Reading: Things to do

1 Write the correct number. Which advertisement is about …

a an activity you can do with your hands? ☐

b activities that can help you earn money? ☐

c an activity that tests your fitness? ☐

d an activity that helps you develop your social skills? ☐

e an activity imported from another country? ☐

Did you know?

Your leisure activities can earn you money!
NEW Courses at Tullyhall College:

2 **Photography for beginners**
Discover the secrets of a perfect photo, from the moment of taking it, through to printing and the best way to show it. You don't need a good camera – you just need a good eye. Is there a professional photographer inside you? Come and find out!

3 **Website design**
How can you share your interests with other people? Where can you meet like-minded people without leaving home? A website opens the door to a world of possibilities. This course can be the start of a money-making career.

4 **Pottery**
Pottery is the art of creating containers and objects out of baked clay. Improve your creativity and make beautiful things for your family and friends.

1

It isn't just a dance. It isn't just a martial art, like Kung-Fu or Tai-kwando. It isn't just exercise.

It's an art form: it's CAPOEIRA
This exciting activity started 400 years ago in Brazil's Bahia region. Capoeira was originally a type of martial art. Slaves used it for self-defence against their masters, but in its modern form there is little physical contact

… and it's here!

Come and test your fitness and strength.

For more information, phone: 0800 345621 or look at our website: www.loncap.com

5 ## Grab the *Limelight!*

Here's a creative activity that's fun and good for your social life

Limelight Workshops develop your social skills through acting, singing and dancing. Soon you will begin to speak more easily and clearly, and become more confident. You will work and play with a group of like-minded adults – and enthusiastic instructors will teach you.

Limelight Workshops

2 Write the answers. The first one is done for you.

What ...

a can help you make a lot of money? *the website design course*

b can make you feel good? ....

c comes from Brazil? ....

d helps you talk to people everywhere? ....

e is for people with no experience? ....

f is more than a dance? ....

g started with slaves? ....

h teaches you to make plates, cups and bowls? ....

i teaches you to use your eyes more carefully? ....

3 Find words in blue from the text for the following meanings.

a the ability to make useful and beautiful things ....

b 100% good ....

c area, part of a country ....

d to do things you like with other people ....

e people with the same opinions as you ....

f They worked for other people. They could not leave because they were not free. ....

g when you feel good about and believe in yourself ....

h when you have cooked something in the oven ....

4 Now replace the underlined words in these sentences with one of the words in blue.

a The trade in <u>owning people to work for you</u> only ended in Nigeria, in 1936.

....

b I've found the <u>ideal</u> place to live, it's just what I want, in every way.

....

c I'm hoping to meet someone <u>with the same opinions as me</u> through Internet dating.

....

d Something went wrong with this cake. Maybe it was <u>cooked in the oven</u> too long.

....

e My writing course gives me an opportunity to express my <u>skill and imagination</u>.

....

f We <u>have the same interests</u> a love for music.

....

g I'm <u>sure of myself</u> – I think I'll do well in the test.

....

●●● B Writing: Designing a poster

1 Look at the poster and answer the questions.

Are you musical? Would you like to be?

Music workshops for people of all levels and ages.

We run classes for beginners in many instruments,
and there's a singing group for anyone who wants to sing.

Saturdays from 9 – 12.30 at Duxton Hall.

For more information ring 17659 39604
www.duxmustart.org.uk

Come and make music! You know you want to!

a What exactly is the poster about? ....
....

b Where does the activity take place? ....
....

c When does the activity take place? ....
....

d How can you find more information? ....
....

e How does the poster say 'it's a good idea'? ....
....

2 Look at the poster again. Which items are in it? Tick the boxes.

a details about money ☐

b details about transport ☐

c details of time and place ☐

d details of who is involved ☐

e colourful pictures ☐

f something to attract your attention ☐

g something to make you want to do it ☐

3 Read the conversation.

I'm thinking of starting a hiking club at the college.

Good idea! Who will it be for?

Anyone who likes the outdoors — and walking!

Will they have to pay anything?

Only their travel costs to and from the area we visit—and their lunch of course!

When will the outings take place?

Every Saturday, starting at 9am. We'll be back by 5pm.

There's a website, www.kings.ac.uk/hiking

How many of the items from exercise 2 are mentioned?

....

....

....

....

....

4 Now use the information to complete the poster.

Do you like .... ?
Come and join our .... !
We'll meet .... , at ....
returning from our hike ....
You only have to pay .... and
.... !
For more information, go to ....

Come on, get your hiking boots on!

●●●A Reading: Why do they do it?

1 Look at the pictures and read the text. Tick the best title for the text.

a Stingray, the King of Surfers ☐

b A Danger-loving Person – are you one? ☐

c The Chemistry of Fear – it's inside your head ☐

d A Wonderful Brain ☐

2 Write the answers to the questions.

a What does Stingray like?

....

b Does Stingray feel fear?

....

c What does Dr Stein say is different in people like Stingray?

....

d What does fear produce in your body?

....

e What do these 'adventurers' need?

....

Meet Stingray. He's a surfer. He likes big waves, big, dangerous waves.

But waves like this can kill you. So why does Stingray surf? What makes him look for danger? Doesn't he feel fear?

Dr Ralph Stein is a psychologist. He studies people like Stingray. He says they do feel fear but they are different from other people. And what is different is the chemistry of their brains.

Dr Stein says the differences in their brain chemistry make them do crazy things. 'They do feel frightened, like most of us,' says Dr Stein. 'What makes them different is what they do about their fear.'

All of our brains make an important chemical called *dopamine*. The difference between 'ordinary people' and these 'adventurers' is that they do not have much dopamine. They look for dangerous situations without thinking. But when they <u>are</u> in danger, they feel fear, just like everybody else. Fear (like anger) makes your body produce *adrenalin*. Adrenalin makes the levels of dopamine go up and this – here's the difference – makes the 'adventurers' feel good. In other words, they look for dangerous situations to make their brain chemistry normal.

'People like this need new and exciting situations all the time', says Dr Stein. 'They are usually friendly and confident, but they get bored easily.' And so, like Stingray, when they see an enormous wave, they don't try to get away from it like most of us do. They swim towards it.

3 Look at the text again. What words does the writer use instead of the words and phrases in *italics*? Write the words.

a Meet Stingray. *Stingray* .... is a surfer.

b *Dr Stein studies people like Stingray.* *Dr Stein* .... says *people like Stingray* .... do feel fear and are not stupid.

4 Find sentences a – e in the text. Who do the underlined pronouns refer to? Circle the best answer, 1 or 2.

a <u>He</u> likes big waves.

  1 surfer

  2 Stingray

b <u>He</u> studies people like Stingray.

  1 Stingray

  2 Dr Stein

c He says <u>they</u> do feel fear.

  1 people like Stingray

  2 people

d In other words, <u>they</u> look for dangerous situations.

  1 levels of dopamine

  2 adventurers

e When they see an enormous wave, they don't try to get away from <u>it</u>.

  1 people like Stingray

  2 the wave

5 Find the adjectives and nouns in the passage to describe these feelings.

a being afraid f _ _ _ _ _ _ _ _

b being very cross _ _ _ e _

c not safe _ _ n _ _ _ _ _

d being sociable and warm towards other people f _ _ _ _ _ _

e being sure of oneself c _ _ _ _ _ _ _ _

f feeling that there is nothing interesting to do _ _ r _ _

●●●B Writing: Organising a paragraph

1 Read the paragraph. Answer the questions that follow.

(1) I just don't understand some people.
(2) They don't say what they mean. (3) For example, the other day I was talking to a friend about the salsa class. (4) She sounded interested so I invited her to come with me. (5) She said 'maybe'. (6) When I called her to confirm she made an excuse. (7) She said 'maybe' but she meant 'no'.

a What is the most important idea in the paragraph (main idea)?

....

Where in the paragraph is this main idea?

....

b What sentences give the main idea?

....

c What sentences explain the main idea?

....

- -

2 Look at the plan and then number these sentences 1 – 6 to make a paragraph.

☐ The other day I was at the cinema.

1 Some people are always talking into their mobile phones.

☐ A mobile phone rang three times during the film.

☐ I hate this.

☐ And the woman answered it every time!

☐ I changed seats, but it was really annoying.

organising a paragraph

main idea
↓
(how you feel about it)
↓
supporting facts and evidence
↓
development of idea
↓
(how you feel about it)
↓
results, if any

3 Look at the picture story and think about what happened.

Now put these sentences into the correct order to make a paragraph. Number them 1 – 10.

a ☐ 1 I was coming out of my drama class one afternoon, wearing my new high-heeled shoes.

b ☐ I looked up and saw a boy, standing with his jeans around his ankles.

c ☐ But coming down some stairs, I lost my balance and started to wobble.

d ☐ I don't know who was more embarrassed then, him or me!

e ☐ Of course, it didn't help, and I fell anyway.

f ☐ As I fell, I grabbed on to someone's legs to stop myself from falling.

g ☐ And suddenly, I knew I was going to fall!

h ☐ It was someone's jeans!

i ☐ I had pulled them down when I fell!

j ☐ But imagine my horror when I saw what I was holding on to.

4 Tick the best title for the paragraph:

a The last time I felt really scared.   ☐

b The last time I felt really proud.   ☐

c The last time I felt really angry.   ☐

d The last time I felt really embarrassed.   ☐

•••A Reading: Fixing it

1 Do you ever have problems with technology? Which of the following is the least helpful thing to do about it?

☐ ask a friend for help

☐ read the instruction manuals

☐ ask the people in the shop where it was bought

☐ get really angry and hit the machine

☐ get help online (on the Internet)

☐ ring a helpline

2 Read the emails quickly. Match the problems and the advice. Write 1, 2 or 3 in the boxes.

A ☐

Dear Steve,
I have a large collection of videos.
They are very important to me. My
VCR is broken and they couldn't
repair it. I couldn't find a new
one in the shops but I managed to
find a combination one (VCR and
DVD player). But what can I do
when they stop making those too?

B ☐

Dear Steve,
I had some old software on my computer. My
friends advised me to buy a program so I did –
even though I could still use my old software
without any problems. I'm not that good with
computers, but I somehow managed to install
it but I still can't use it properly. What can I do?
I couldn't understand the online tutorial at all.

C ☐

Dear Steve,
My father has a valuable collection of records
but he can't play them any more. He prefers
the sound of old-fashioned vinyl records, so
CDs are out. I want to buy him a record player
for his birthday. Can you still buy them?

Are you having problems with technology?

*I'm Steve and I am here to help you.
No problem is too big or too small. Just email your
question and I'll get right back to you. It's that simple.*

steve@teknoprobs.com

1 Dear Mark,
It's time to change your technology.
Choose your best videos and record them
onto DVDs. 'Precious moments' on
Clarence Road have a special service.
They can even add music and
commentary to your film!

2 Dear Juanita,
A few years ago you could find secondhand record players easily. Now they can
be quite difficult to find. I managed to buy
one on the Internet recently. Try one of the
websites for secondhand equipment, like
www.wozwunce.com

3 Dear Susanna,
Get a personal tutor or take a computer
class. It's expensive but it is worth it. You
can find a tutor in the local newspaper and
the local college has lots of computer
classes at all levels.

3 Read the emails again quickly. Write names and advice in the blanks.

a the name of a place to record videos onto DVDs ....

b a good way to learn to use a computer ....

c a good place to find equipment that is not made any more ....

d a problem caused by new technology ....

e something that can help you use your software correctly ....

4 Read the emails more carefully. Answer the questions.

a 'They are very important to me.' *What* is very important? ....

b 'Now they can be very difficult to find.' *What* can be difficult to find? ....

c 'I somehow managed to install it ...' *What* did he manage to install? ....

d '... and record them onto DVDs.' Record *what* onto DVDs? ....

e 'I want to buy him a record player ...' Buy *who* a record player? ....

f 'Can you still buy them?' Buy *what*? ....

5 Look at the words in blue in the text. Match them with the definitions.

a to make a broken object good again (v) ....

b not new [used by someone else before you (adj)] ....

c a set of similar things put together (n) ....

d worth a lot of money (adj) ....

e to connect a piece of equipment and make it ready to use (v) ....

f not modern (adj) ....

g in a correct way (adv) ....

h to be able to do something difficult after trying hard (v) ....

6 Now use the words in blue to complete the sentences.

a That old record might be quite .... by now. You should try selling it to an antique shop.

b I don't think my computer is working .... Every time I try to save a document, it crashes.

c Can you tell me how to .... this new software on my computer?

d Wow! Your CD .... is really impressive. You must have about 400!

e They don't make this kind of cassette recorder any more, but you might find an old one in a .... shop.

f Look at this wonderful .... record player from the 1920s.

g I've been looking everywhere for a copy of this rare CD, but so far, I haven't .... to find it.

h My printer is broken, but it costs too much to .... I may as well buy a new one.

B Writing: Using pronouns

1 Read the paragraph. What is wrong with it?

Technology drives me crazy because I am not very good with technology. For example, I use the computer all the time but I can't use the computer well. All my friends are surprised because all my friends use their computers all the time. I'm going to take a course and surprise all my friends even more!

....
....
....
....
....
....
....
....
....

2 Write *it*, *they*, or *them* for the underlined words in the text.

a technology ....

b the computer ....

c 'because all my friends' ....

d 'surprise all my friends' ....

3 Rewrite these paragraphs. Use pronouns to avoid repetition.

a A lot of people hate answering machines but I love answering machines. I've got an answering machine at home. As soon as I get home I turn my answering machine on and listen to the messages on my answering machine. My answering machine is also useful because I can hear who is calling and only answer if I want to.

....
....
....
....
....
....
....
....
....

b Mariella can't live without her hairdryer. Mariella uses her hairdryer every day because Mariella thinks her looks are very important. Mariella even took her hairdryer when we went camping but the batteries were flat and of course Mariella couldn't plug her hairdryer in anywhere.

....
....
....
....
....
....
....
....

4 What do the underlined pronouns in this text refer to? Write the nouns in the spaces.

Technology is now part of everyone's lives. <u>It</u> is part of <u>our</u> jobs, our leisure time, home life and even our clothing. Designers are always coming up with new ideas. A few years ago, in Japan, <u>they</u> made the first "wearable PC". <u>It</u> was also known as the MP3 jacket. <u>This</u> had a built-in computer, mobile phone and a micro-recorder in <u>its</u> pocket. Imagine ... <u>your</u> boss has called you to a boring meeting with <u>him</u> and your colleagues. <u>They</u> would never realise that you weren't listening to <u>them</u>, but to your favourite music instead ....

a It ....

f its ....

b our ....

g your ....

c they ....

h him ....

d It ....

i They ....

e This ....

j them ....

5 Rewrite the sentences below to make a paragraph. Try to use pronouns wherever possible, instead of repeating words.

a There's a new mobile phone on the market.
b I really want one of the mobile phones.
c With the new mobile phones it's possible to make videos.
d First, you film something.
e Then you send it to your friend.
f Within seconds, your friend can see the same thing as you have just seen!
g This technology is amazing.
h This technology gets better all the time.
i There'll be a new type of phone on the market in a few months.
j I suppose I'll want the new type of mobile phone then, too.

....

....

....

....

....

....

....

....

....

....

....

....

A Singapore

'When people give you presents you don't open them right then. That looks as if you really need or want them! It's better to wait until later!'

●●●A Reading: Culture clash

1 Read about the countries. Write the names of the countries where you:

a kiss 'hello' once only ....

b don't take 6, 8 or 10 flowers ....

c don't open presents straight away. ....

- -

2 Read the introduction.

Alice is reading her emails. Three of them are from three different friends. The friends are volunteers in different countries. That means they are working because they want to, but they are not being paid.

B Argentina

'In my country we kiss 'hello' on the cheek once, but we don't really touch. It's different from France and other places where they kiss two or three times.'

Now read the emails. Complete the sentences which follow.

a Joanna is in .... She made a mistake because she

....

b Anthony is in .... He made a mistake because he

....

c Naomi is in .... She made a mistake because she

....

C Poland

'There's this old idea in my country. When you take flowers you must take an odd number (3, 5, 7, etc.), not an even number (2, 4, 6, etc.). Something to do with luck I think.'

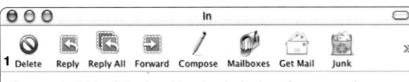

1 Delete   Reply   Reply All   Forward   Compose   Mailboxes   Get Mail   Junk

Guess what! Mrs S the head teacher invited me for supper. I was really nervous so I took some flowers as a present. When I gave them to her she looked at them and counted them – I think! Do you think that's possible? Then she smiled and said it was nice of me. But there was something wrong. The dinner was great, though. And at the weekend we're going skiing. It's my first time but I'm really looking forward to it!
I miss you all.
Joanna XXX

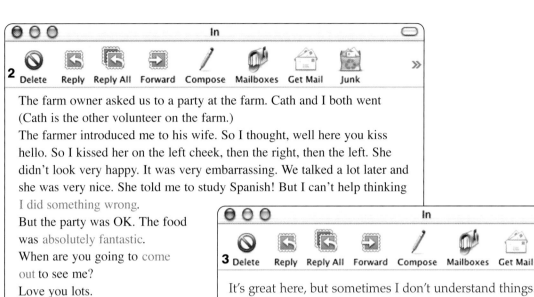

In

2 Delete | Reply | Reply All | Forward | Compose | Mailboxes | Get Mail | Junk

The farm owner asked us to a party at the farm. Cath and I both went
(Cath is the other volunteer on the farm.)
The farmer introduced me to his wife. So I thought, well here you kiss
hello. So I kissed her on the left cheek, then the right, then the left. She
didn't look very happy. It was very embarrassing. We talked a lot later and
she was very nice. She told me to study Spanish! But I can't help thinking
I did something wrong.
But the party was OK. The food
was absolutely fantastic.
When are you going to come
out to see me?
Love you lots.
Anthony

In

3 Delete | Reply | Reply All | Forward | Compose | Mailboxes | Get Mail | Junk

It's great here, but sometimes I don't understand things. Take last
night, for example. Terry and I invited some people from the medical
centre for drinks.
They all arrived at the same time. I offered them drinks, then I gave the
wrong drinks to the wrong people. Ouch! But they didn't mind that.
Two of them brought us presents. One was a silver key-ring, and
another was a really nice pen. But when we opened them everyone
looked at the floor. In silence. Imagine! Did we do something wrong? I
mean… it was only for a second and the rest of the evening was great
fun. Strange. Terry says I'm being silly.
Love to all at the flat. I'll see you in six weeks. Can't wait.
Naomi.

3 Write the names of the person who:

a cooks really well ....

b didn't say anything for a minute or two
....

c has a nice wife ....

d is a volunteer in a medical centre
....

e is a volunteer in a school ....

f is a volunteer on a farm ....

g organised a successful evening ....

h was worried about the invitation
....

i works with Anthony ....

4 Find words and phrases in blue in the emails.
Write them next to their definitions below.

a I made a mistake, but I don't know what.
I did something wrong ....

b I'm going to tell you a typical story about last
night. ....

c It's in the future. I'm enthusiastic about it.
....

d Really, really, really good.
....

e Something wasn't right. I don't know what.
....

f They weren't cross or unhappy.
....

g (You) travel to my place for a visit.
....

h You keep your keys on one of these.
....

B Writing: 'thank you' letters, emails & txt

1 Match the 'thank you' messages to the pictures.
Write **a** – **b** in the boxes.

a Hey, about the party. Great. I'll be there. ☐

b Hi Carol,
Thanks for invite. I'd love to.
See you tomorrow.
Matt ☐

c Dear Mr and Mrs Jordan,
Thank you for the invitation to your party
on December 23. We would love to come.
With best wishes,
John and Brian ☐

d Thx 4 invite. I'll b there. CU 2moro. ☐

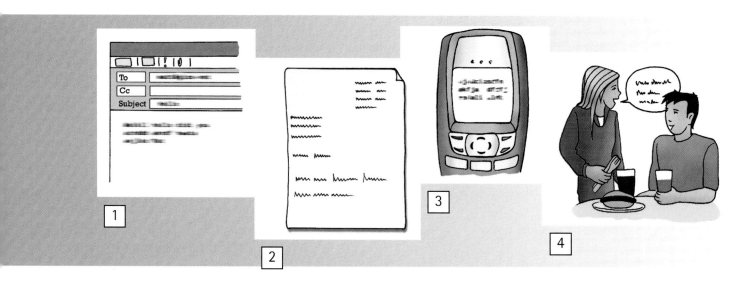

2 Which of the messages are formal? Which are informal?

a ....

b ....

c ....

d ....

3 In exercise 1 everybody says 'yes'. Here are some 'no' answers.
   Which pictures (1 – 4) are they for? Write 1 – 4 in the boxes.

   a Can't come. Nxt wk? ☐

   b 'Fraid I can't make it. Sorry. See you around. ☐

   c I'm afraid I can't make it. What a pity! But let's get together soon. ☐

   d I'm afraid we won't be able to come, but I hope we'll see you soon. ☐

4 Complete the email. Choose the most appropriate language.

	In	
1 Delete Reply Reply All Forward Compose Mailboxes Get Mail Junk		

Dear Catherine,

.... that you've moved into our street.
.... to a drinks party to get to know some of the
other neighbours. .... ?
.... number 25, at the other end of the street.
Hope to see you,

....

Sally and Bob Mills

a 1 It's brilliant
   2 We're so pleased

b 1 We'd like to invite you
   2 We must get you over

c 1 Wanna come?
   2 Would you like to come?

d 1 Our place is
   2 We live at

e 1 Cheers, mate
   2 With best wishes

5 Look at the following invitations. Say if they are formal or
   informal. How do you know?

   a ....

   b ....

   c ....

6 Reply to the following invitations. Say 'no' or 'yes'.

   a
   | Hi Kate
   We're having a party on
   Saturday. Do you want to
   come? About 8?
   David |

   a (say yes) ....
   ....
   ....
   ....

   b
   | Can u meet 4
   dinner 2moro
   eve? C |

   b (say no) ....
   ....
   ....
   ....

   c
   Dear Matthew,
   I am writing to invite you to a
   dinner party on Saturday
   January 15th. I do hope you
   will be able to come.
   Best wishes
   Sarah

   c (say no) ....
   ....
   ....
   ....

...A Reading: Caroline

1 Complete the table about the person in the text.

In their own words

Caroline Rippin, 30, actor

Most actors say that drama school is one of the best times of your life because you act *all the time*. You train and study all day and you often rehearse in the evenings, practising for the next day's show. That doesn't happen in your life as an actor.

When I was twelve or thirteen, one of my teachers – she was called Candy – talked to my parents. She said 'send your daughter to acting school – to a drama school. She's going to be a good actor.' I really wanted to go to drama school too, but my parents said 'No, finish <u>this</u> school first.' And they were right. I got a normal education and then I went to drama school.

I'm a theatre actor. I've done a bit of TV, and I do other things, but theatre is where I feel most 'at home'. But I'm lucky because I don't just act in the theatre, I also direct a schools' theatre group. We go into schools and make shows together with the kids. They help us write the dramas. We do plays about difficult topics for kids. It's easier for them to talk about difficult topics through drama.

Some actors find it very difficult to learn their lines – the words. It's not difficult for me. I don't learn my lines before I go to the first rehearsal. I learn the lines at the same time as I learn how to act the play.

I've never forgotten my lines during a play, but some actors do. I worked in a play once and the actor forgot his lines so he just kept saying the same line again and again. I looked at his face. He was really frightened - terrified! But he remembered in the end. The audience didn't notice anything!

When I'm not working – when I don't have any acting work – I keep fit and do exercises for my voice. My voice is the most important thing I've got.

I relax by listening to music. I like a lot of different music – jazz, blues, soul.

My favourite smell is watermelon.

Name:	
Age:	
Occupation:	
Where she does it:	
Favourite music:	
Favourite smell:	

INTERVIEWED BY PETER HEDLEY

2 Write answers to the questions.

a Who didn't want Caroline to go to stage school? ....

b What do drama students do in the evenings? ....

c What does Caroline do in schools? ....

d Who got a normal education? ....

e What is the best time of your life? ....

f Who learns lines in rehearsal? ....

g Who wanted Caroline to go to drama school? ....

h Who was terrified? ....

3 Match the words from the text (on the left) with the meanings on the right.

a audience	1 actors have to learn these – the words of a play	a 6	f ....
b direct		b	g ....
c drama school	2 any kind of music or acting event on a stage	c	h ....
d fit	3 strong, healthy; can do a lot of exercise	d	i ....
e lines	4 students learn about acting in one of these	e	j ....
f rehearse	5 subjects, themes		
g relax	6 they watch a show		
h show	7 to tell actors what to do		
i topics	8 to do something easy; to rest		
j train	9 to learn how to do something		
	10 to practise a play again and again before the first night		

4 Read the text again and guess what questions Caroline was asked in each paragraph.

a What is it like at drama school? ....

b ....

c ....

d ....

e ....

f ....

g ....

h ....

B Writing: In their own words

1 Match the questions and the answers. Write 1 – 9 in the boxes.

a What were you like as a child? ☐

b When did you first learn another language? ☐

c What is one of your happiest memories as a child? ☐

d Who was your first love? ☐

e What kind of music do you like? ☐

f What do you do in your free time? ☐

g What would you say is the biggest problem facing the world? ☐

h What's your favourite food? ☐

i What smell reminds you of home? ☐

1 Living together in peace.

2 Classical music, at the moment. I've just 'discovered' it, and I love it. In the past I thought it was boring, can you believe that!

3 I'm learning to play the guitar, and when I'm not practising, I like going out with my friends, dancing, eating good food, watching our local team play football.

4 I remember my parents took me to a fun fair when I was about six. The sounds, the ice cream, the excitement and fear I felt – it was unforgettable.

5 I was quiet and serious. You'd never believe it, looking at me now!

6 Italian food. I can't get enough of it – all those delicious pizzas, pastas, fish dishes – and ice cream! Nobody makes ice cream like the Italians.

7 My neighbour, when I was about four! We used to play together in a tree house. I thought I'd marry him. But I haven't seen him again since I was about seven.

8 The smell of roses. My mother used to grow them in our garden. It's such a romantic smell. Whenever I smell roses now, I think of her.

9 When I was at secondary school, we all had to learn French or English. I'm glad we were forced to learn another language, because otherwise, I would never have realised what fun it is, speaking to someone from another country, in his / her own language.

In their own words

2 Read the interview notes about Tom. What were the questions?
Write the interview. Use the interview in exercise 1 as a model.

age: will be 25 in a week's time!

grew up in small town in south west Scotland.

childhood: riding bikes in the woods, building tree houses, swimming in the lakes

studies: went to university in Edinburgh, (English and Spanish)

first job: teaching English in Peru, 3 years ago

best things: the Peruvian people, the food, the mountains — and the music.

most memorable experience: climbing up Machu Picchu at sunrise — magical

wants to travel to other countries (China, Japan, India).

Eventually hopes to settle back in Scotland (start language school there)

...A Reading: The people quiz

1 Read the text. Match the paragraphs with the pictures. Write the correct paragraph number (1 – 5) in the boxes.

Craig Newmark (1953–)

Ian Wilmut (with Dolly) (1944–)

Wangari Maathai (1940–)

DO YOU KNOW THESE PEOPLE?

Who are the people described below?

Try our quiz.

1 This man is a biologist from Scotland. The first ever clone of a mammal was grown by him – a sheep named Dolly. As a child he wanted to be a farmer, but one summer when he was working in a laboratory he became interested in cells and animals.

2 On December 10, 1997, this woman climbed into a Redwood tree that is 55 metres (180 feet) tall. Some people wanted to cut the 1000-year-old tree down and destroy it, but she wanted to protect it.

  She came down from the tree on December 18, 1999. While she was in the tree (she called the [...]na'), people from all over the world became [...]ed in her, because of the way she was [...]ng the forest. She has inspired thousands [...]e to help protect the environment.

3 In 1995, this man started an online bulletin board where people could post messages on almost any subject in his hometown of San Francisco. The idea was very popular and there are now Craigslists in over 100 cities in North and South America, Europe, Asia and Australia. On Craigslists you can look for a place to live, you can look for a job, you can buy and sell things, or you can just post a message and read replies to your message.

4 In 2002, this young chef started a cooking school for young people. The school was for people who were unemployed and had problems in their lives. The well-known chef started a new restaurant and the 'difficult' students at the school were then given jobs there. Every year a group of young unemployed people study at the school. They are all inspired by this chef.

5 This environmentalist is from Kenya and won the Nobel Peace Prize in 2004 for her work for human rights and the environment. In 1976 she started a movement called 'The Green Belt Movement' which plants trees to protect the environment and to improve life in Africa. 20 million trees have been planted since 1976.

2 Write the words from the box in the blanks.

a A group of people. They want to change things. ....

b Scientists work in one of these. ....

c The air, water, and earth; we live in it. ....

d They are animals. They drink their mother's milk. ....

e They study plants and animals. ....

f To make someone feel excited and confident. ....

biologists	environment
inspire	laboratory
mammals	movement

Julia "Butterfly" Hill (1974–)   Jamie Oliver (1975–)

3 Read the text again. Who or what …

a was Dolly? ....

b is 'Luna'? ....

c is a Craigslist? ....

d is for people who have had problems in their lives? ....

e plants trees? ....

f wants to protect the environment? ....

4 Complete these sentences with one of the words in blue from the texts.

a When you ride a motorcycle you wear a helmet to .... your head.

b He is a great .... The food he makes looks good and is delicious.

c This animal is exactly the same as that one – in fact it looks like a ....

d They want to .... the building because it is dangerous. Now they are going to build a new, safer building.

e Please put your message on this .... Then everyone can see it.

f All living things are made up of ....

g All people have .... These are the basic things that we expect, like the right to live and the right to work.

h I don't have a job, so I am ....

●●●B Writing: Opinion emails

1 Read emails 1 and 2.

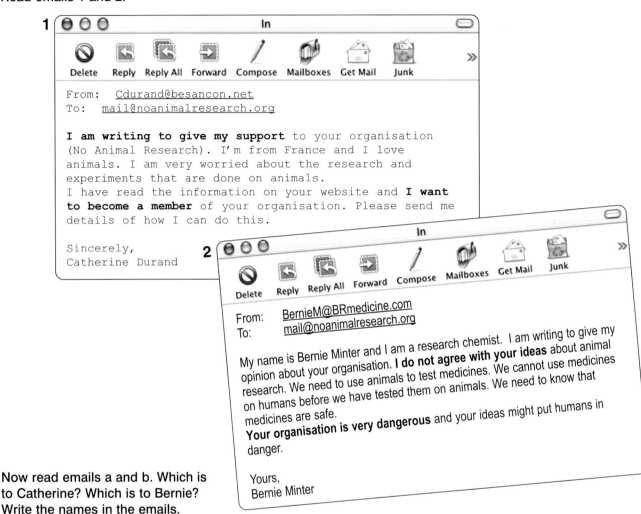

1

In

Delete Reply Reply All Forward Compose Mailboxes Get Mail Junk

From: Cdurand@besancon.net
To: mail@noanimalresearch.org

I am writing to give my support to your organisation
(No Animal Research). I'm from France and I love
animals. I am very worried about the research and
experiments that are done on animals.
I have read the information on your website and **I want
to become a member** of your organisation. Please send me
details of how I can do this.

Sincerely,
Catherine Durand

2

In

Delete Reply Reply All Forward Compose Mailboxes Get Mail Junk

From: BernieM@BRmedicine.com
To: mail@noanimalresearch.org

My name is Bernie Minter and I am a research chemist. I am writing to give my
opinion about your organisation. **I do not agree with your ideas** about animal
research. We need to use animals to test medicines. We cannot use medicines
on humans before we have tested them on animals. We need to know that
medicines are safe.
Your organisation is very dangerous and your ideas might put humans in
danger.

Yours,
Bernie Minter

Now read emails a and b. Which is
to Catherine? Which is to Bernie?
Write the names in the emails.

a

In

Delete Reply Reply All Forward Compose Mailboxes Ge

From: Jenny Morgan [j.morgan@noanimalresearch.org]

Dear .... ,
Thank you for your email. We respect your opinions as
a scientist, but we do not agree with you. Animal
research is not necessary. Please look at our website
www.noanimalresearch.org for more information.
Best regards,
Jenny Morgan
Publicity Manager

b

In

Delete Reply Reply All Forward Compose Mailboxes Get Mail Junk

No Animal Research
From: Marshall Kingsley
[m.kingsley@noanimalresearch.org]

Dear .... ,

Thank you very much for your email. It is very
easy to become a member of No Animal Research
and you can do this online. You need to fill in
a form and give us your credit card number.
Please see www.noanimalresearch.org for details.

Kind regards,
Marshall Kingsley
Assistant Director
No Animal Research

2   Read emails 1 and 2 again. Which of the expressions in bold are used to show that you are in favour of (for) the organisation? Which expressions show that you are against the organisation? Complete the table.

For	Against
I am writing to give my support.	

3   Write an email to the organisation 'No Animal Research'. Write for or against. Use arguments from the table.

In favour	Against
Animals cannot protect themselves – we need to defend them.	Humans need animals for food and for clothing.
Animals have feelings and feel pain.	Animals are not as important as humans.
It is not necessary to test cosmetics on animals.	Animals do not have rights.

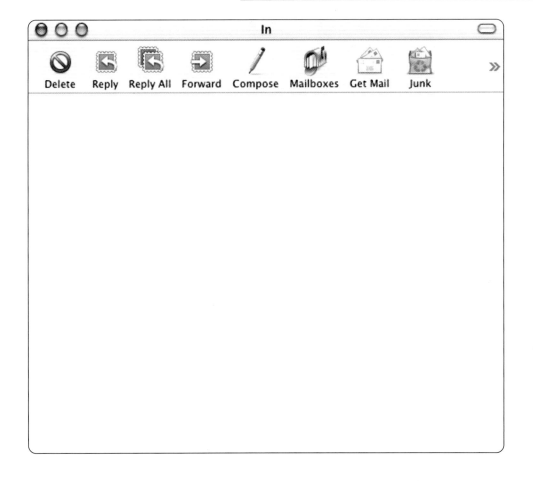

•••A Reading: Being intelligent in different ways

1 Read the article about different types of intelligence. Write the name of the appropriate intelligence next to the photographs of famous European and American people.

a

b

c

d

David Beckham: soccer player

....

Albert Einstein: physicist

....

William Shakespeare: writer

....

Jane Goodall: primatologist

....

e

f

g

h

i

Ludwig van Beethoven: composer

....

Oprah Winfrey: talk show host

....

Anne Frank: diarist

....

Frank Lloyd Wright: architect

....

Rev. Martin Luther King: spiritual leader

....

It's not 'how clever are you?', it's 'how are you clever?'

This week's article looks at a great theory and gives you the chance to find your own talents and what you could study. Read on ...

In 1983, Dr Howard Gardner first said that there is more than one way to be intelligent. Dr Gardner says that we all have a lot of <u>different</u> intelligences – *Multiple* Intelligences. Read on and find out what those intelligences are.

- Are you good at learning languages? Do you love to read and write? If the answer is 'yes' to these two questions, you have high linguistic intelligence; the ability to use language.

- What about numbers? Are you quick at doing sums? If so, you probably have high logical–mathematical intelligence – the talent for understanding logic and for using numbers.

- Do you see things in your head? No, you're not crazy, but you probably do have high spatial intelligence. You are probably good at reading maps and understanding diagrams. You probably also remember things using images, colours and pictures.

- How are you on the dance floor? Are you good at sports and dancing? Kinesthetic intelligence is the talent for using your body well to move or to show emotion.

- Do you sing in the shower? Play any musical instruments? Yes? You probably have high musical intelligence – the ability to hear, recognise and remember music.

- Do you love working in teams? Do you have a lot of friends? You probably have high interpersonal intelligence. This is the talent for understanding other people's thoughts and feelings.

- Do you keep a diary? Do you think about your own character and actions a lot? You may have high intrapersonal intelligence. This means you are good at understanding yourself and are self-aware.

- 'To be or not to be' – this is the question for those with high existential intelligence: this is about being able to understand things that are spiritual and things that relate to the meaning of life and death.

And finally:

- Do you like to spend time with nature? Do you have pets? Do you like to grow plants? If so, you probably have high naturalistic intelligence – the talent for understanding how natural things in the world work.

So, how are <u>you</u> intelligent? We hope this article has helped you to find out.

2 **Complete this table of word families using words from the text.**

a language	linguistic
b logic	
c mathematics	
d space	
e kinesthetics	
f music	
g person	
h existence	
i nature	

B Writing: Writing about myself

1   Read the text. Match the paragraphs and the topics in the box.

Please tell us about yourself here:

I think I am a sociable, confident person. I get on well with other people and I have a lot of close friends. I love to work with others and I also love animals. I grew up with animals, because my father is a vet and my mother breeds dogs.

I am a very active person and I have a lot of outdoor hobbies, like walking and climbing. I also love playing sports, especially volleyball and hockey, and I love dancing. I play the piano and sing in a choir.

My other hobby is travelling. Last year I visited South America for a month and this year I'm going to go to India for the first time. I enjoy travel because it gives me the chance to meet other people and to get to know other cultures.

Paragraph 1 ....

Paragraph 2 ....

Paragraph 3 ....

Interests and activities
Travel
Personality

---

2   Are the following statements about Carmen true (T) or false (F)?

a She does not have many friends. ☐

b Her parents both work with animals. ☐

c Carmen likes to be outside. ☐

d She is a musical person. ☐

e She has been to India. ☐

3   Look at the questions. Which paragraph (1, 2 or 3) has the answer? Write the number of the paragraph in the boxes.

Now write the answers to the questions.

a Why does Carmen like to visit other places? ☐

....

....

b What is Carmen like? ☐

....

....

c What are Carmen's main hobbies? ☐

....

....

4 Now read about Robert and complete the form for him.

Please tell us about yourself here:

Robert McInnes

Personal characteristics:

- quiet, serious
- a good listener
- sense of humour

Interests:

- photography
- writing poetry (wrote book of poems, published last year)
- music (play the violin in an orchestra)

Sports:

mountain climbing, hiking, sailing

Future plans:

travel to Africa to do wildlife photography

DESCRIBING THINGS

•••A Reading: Zaha Hadid

1 Look at the web page. Complete the table as quickly as possible.

FIRSTS

Who is Zaha Hadid? by Peter Hedley

What does a famous architect look like? Well, he's normally quite old with white hair. He often looks rather serious. Sometimes he wears modern glasses (the latest fashion), and grey suits. He comes from England, the USA, Germany, Japan or Spain.

But not Zaha Hadid. Firstly, she's a woman. And then she grew up in Iraq before she went to London as a student. Zaha, who is not a quiet person, is passionate about what she does. In the words of writer Christopher Hawthorne, she is 'a big woman with a bigger intellect and a gigantic personality'. She wears fashionable clothes, bright shiny jewellery, and very high-heeled shoes. When she's excited she rolls her eyes, and shouts at the students and colleagues who work with her. But the same colleagues and friends say that she is 'good with people'; it's just that she cares, really cares about architecture. As one of her friends says, when you get to know Zaha Hadid, you realize that all the storms are on the outside – the weather may be bad the other side of the window, but in the house it's all calm and peaceful!

But it hasn't always been easy for Zaha Hadid. In 1994, she won a competition for a new opera house in Cardiff, Wales (UK). The public weren't interested, however. They said they wanted a new sports stadium, not the opera house and so her design (see picture) was never built. But other people were noticing her work and suddenly she was designing buildings all over the world (like the Museum of Contemporary Art in Cincinnati, USA) and winning prizes.

In the newspapers they call Zaha the 'diva of contemporary architecture' – as if she was a bad-tempered opera star. Zaha Hadid's reply? 'Would they call me a diva if I was a guy?'

Home | people A – Z | back to the top
Today's news | Contact us | Help

The Vitra Fire Station in Germany, one of Zaha Hadid's first public buildings

A model for the Cardiff opera house. They never built it!

Name:	
Country of origin:	
Occupation:	
Type of character:	

2   Find the words from the text in blue. Write them in the correct blanks.

    a   a place for public football, athletics, etc. ....

    b   a very successful female singer, easily annoyed ....

    c   easily annoyed ....

    d   is really interested in something and wants it to be good ....

    e   making drawings and pictures for new buildings ....

    f   modern, of the present time ....

    g   moves her eyes around to show that she is not happy ....

    h   very, very big ....

    i   the power of the mind to think and learn ....

    j   with very strong feelings or ideas about something ....

3   Now use the words in blue (changing the form if necessary) to complete the sentences.

    a   What a naughty little girl. Did you see how she .... when her mother scolded her?

    b   I've always been .... about playing a musical instrument, and as soon as I can afford it, I'm going to buy a piano.

    c   Ayers Rock, or Uluru, as it's now called, is a .... rock in the desert in Australia.

    d   The professor is a person of great .... and wisdom.

    e   Unless I have a cup of coffee in the morning, I become very .... !

    f   Norman Foster is the architect who .... the new Wembley stadium.

    g   They are starting to build the enormous .... that will house the Olympic Games in London in 2012.

    h   He really .... for animals, so he has decided to become a vet.

    i   Monica Ali is one of Britain's best writers of .... fiction.

    j   Some people say that the young soul singer, Joss Stone, is just a good as that great .... , Aretha Franklin.

4   Read the text again and answer the following questions.

    a   Why is Zaha Hadid different from other architects? (Think of at least three reasons.)

       ....

       ....

    b   Where did Zaha Hadid study? ....

    c   What is Christopher Hawthorne's opinion of Zaha's intelligence and personality?

       ....

    d   How do we know that Zaha Hadid is passionate?

       ....

    e   What did Zaha Hadid win, and what happened next?

       ....

       ....

●●● B Writing: Descriptive paragraph

1 **Read the descriptions. Which one describes the photo?**

a It's one of the most beautiful buildings in London. It is two hundred and fifty years old. It is tall and white. It looks very peaceful, and it is a friendly building. Every time I go there I feel happy.

b It's one of the most exciting sights in London. It was built in 2004. It is tall and very dramatic. You can see it from miles away. It looks like a gigantic vegetable, and so some people call it 'the Gherkin'.

c It's one of the ugliest buildings in London. It is only a few years old. It is wide and rather fat. It looks like a tomato. It's next to some beautiful old buildings, so it doesn't look right.

2 **Make a list of all the adjectives used to describe the buildings in the texts.**

3 **Which ones are used to convey a positive impression? Which ones convey a negative impression? Write them in the table.**

Adjective	Positive	Negative

4 **Look at each paragraph, and find sentences about:**

age	description	extra information	opening sentence
Text **a**	Text **a**	Text **a**	Text **a**
Text **b**	Text **b**	Text **b**	Text **b**
Text **c**	Text **c**	Text **c**	Text **c**

5 Look at the photograph below. Use the notes to write a paragraph about it, under the following headings.

Built in 2004

Edinburgh

Designer: Spanish architect Enric Mirales

'The roof looks like an upside down boat.'

'It looks like a swimming pool, a big superstore warehouse and a public car park, all put together.'

'I can't believe it won an architecture award. It should get a prize for being the ugliest building in Britain.'

'It looks like something a three-year-old would make out of Lego.'

'What are those things on the windows? Hammers? Curtains? Hairdryers?'

'I think it's great – modern, European and forward-looking.'

How old it is ....

Where it is ....

What's special about it (very old, very new, beautiful, ugly, etc.) ....

....

....

What it looks like ....

....

How you feel about it ....

....

Any other information about it ....

....

6 Use the paragraph structure table opposite to write a paragraph about the building. You can use the sample language in the table and find more in the notes.

Paragraph Structure	Sample language
General opening sentence	One of the .... buildings in .... is ....
▼	
Facts about the building (age, etc.)	It is .... years old. It was built in ....
▼	
What it looks like	
▼	
What I think about it	

•••▶A Reading: A good night's sleep

1 Read the text. Complete the table with the four things that stop people from sleeping. For each thing, say why it stops people from sleeping.

Things that stop us from sleeping				
Why?				

Are you getting enough sleep?

Many doctors say today that sleep can change our health. If we want our bodies to work well, we need sleep. If people don't have enough sleep, they can suffer from depression as well as illnesses such as heart disease.

The most obvious effect of not having enough sleep is to make us weaker and it makes it harder to fight illness; in other words, people who do not sleep enough are more likely to get sick or ill.

Many people have sleeping problems. Studies in the USA have found that 60 per cent of adults have problems sleeping a lot of the time. More than 40 per cent of adults say that they feel sleepy in the daytime and that this makes their lives difficult.

20 per cent say they sometimes have problems sleeping. At least 40 million people in the USA suffer from sleep problems that need treatment – because they sleep too much or too little – but very few people actually go to a doctor about their sleep problem.

So what are the things that affect sleep? Well, firstly, there's noise. If there are noises such as barking dogs, dripping taps and loud music, you'll probably find it difficult to sleep. What is interesting is that women seem to notice noise more than men, while young children do not notice noise as much as adults.

If you are sitting in a chair, you'll find it very difficult to sleep. But you will probably have no problem falling asleep if you are lying down. This is another thing that affects sleep – sleep surface. We need to be horizontal and we need to have enough space.

A third thing affecting sleep is temperature. You may have noticed that you have difficulty sleeping if it is very hot or cold. Studies have found that if the temperature is below 12°C or above 24°C, we will wake up. Altitude too, can change the way we sleep. If you are at an altitude of over 4,000 m, you need to breathe differently because you don't have as much oxygen. It will take you about two weeks to get used to this. So, if you want to sleep well:

• Do not do exercise before you go to bed.
• Do not drink alcohol or drinks like coffee that have caffeine.
• Do try to relax.

We hope this helps. Sleep well.

2 Read the passage again. Complete the following sentences. Circle the best word or phrase (1, 2 or 3).

a Not having enough sleep …
1 can cause illness.
2 does not change health.
3 makes us stronger.

b The number of adults who say that they often have problems trying to fall asleep is …
1 40%.
2 20%.
3 60%.

c The people who notice noise most are …
1 men.
2 women.
3 babies.

d At high altitudes we need to breathe …
1 without oxygen.
2 less oxygen.
3 differently.

e Before you go to bed, you should NOT …
1 listen to relaxing music.
2 drink coffee without caffeine.
3 go for a two-kilometre run.

3 Look at the words in blue from the text. Write them in the correct blanks.

a a gas that people need to breathe ....

b completely flat, lying down ....

c an illness. It makes you feel very unhappy ....

d to see, hear or feel something ....

e given to someone who is ill to make them get better ....

f something found in, for example, coffee that makes the body work faster ....

g how high you are above sea level ....

4 Now use the words in blue to complete these sentences.

a He is in hospital now. They're giving him .... to help him breathe more easily.

b The best .... for a cold is to lie in bed with a hot water bottle.

c The seats in first class on planes can go backwards so that you can lie in an almost .... position.

d This is a very sad song. I believe the singer was suffering from .... when he wrote it.

e When I was mountain climbing in Peru, I felt quite ill from the high ....

f Coffee, and even tea and fizzy drinks contain ....

g At first I found the traffic noise on this street unbearable, but now I hardly .... it.

B Writing: Ordering important ideas

1 Which of these things do you think are important for good health? Complete the table with your order. Write 1 – 10 (1 = very important, 10 = not very important)

	My order	Marco's order
a enough sleep		
b good food		
c hobbies		
d friends		
e plenty of money		
f regular medical check-ups		
g people who care about you		
h a nice place to live		
i regular exercise		
j interesting work		

2 Now write the ideas under the correct headings.

Diet and fitness

....*a*..............................

Home life

....

Money

....

Social life

.... 🔑

3 Read this essay written by Marco. What order do you think he would have for the things in exercise 1? Complete the table.

If you want to stay healthy, there are many things that you can do. The first one is to eat and sleep well. I try to sleep at least eight hours every night and I try to eat a balanced diet. I go to see a doctor once a year for a check-up and I exercise twice a week.

It is also good for your health if you have good friends and people who care about you. You need to have people to go out with and things that interest you. If you have hobbies, this will also help you to have a healthy lifestyle.

Where you live and where you work are also important to your lifestyle. If you have a good job and a comfortable home, you will stay healthy. I am a student of medicine and I live with two friends in a nice house. This helps me a lot.

The least important thing for good health is having a lot of money. If you have a lot of money, this won't stop you from getting sick, but of course it helps you to have a more comfortable life. There are many times that I can't afford to buy the things that I want, but because I have the other things, I don't really mind.

.... 🔑

4 Read Marco's essay again. Match the paragraphs with the headings in exercise 2.

Paragraph 1: ....

Paragraph 2: ....

Paragraph 3: ....

Paragraph 4: ....

5 Add the following sentences to the correct paragraphs in the essay.

That doesn't mean I go to the gym or run around the park; yoga is also good for you, physically as well as mentally, and that's what I do once a week, at home.

And if you are new to a place, a great way of making new friends is to find something interesting to do or learn.

It's nice to be able to talk about things to people when you come home.

I know a lot of rich people who aren't happy at all.

A paragraph has got three main parts:
The opening sentence. It should catch the reader's attention and introduce the topic of the paragraph.
The body of the paragraph. These sentences add more detail and give more information about the topic.
The closing sentence. This acts as a summary of the whole paragraph.

6 Circle the best opening sentence and closing sentence for this topic: Keeping fit

Opening sentences
a Good diet is the most important factor in being healthy.
b Nobody can deny that fitness is essential for health.
c If you are unfit, you won't feel good, or look good either.

Closing sentences
a If you do regular exercise, and eat well, you'll be fit and healthy.
b Give up fast food and drink in moderation.
c It's difficult to have energy when you aren't fit.

7 Read Marco's essay again, and underline the words that introduce the topic in the opening line of each paragraph. The first one has been done for you.

•••A Reading: Burning man

1 Read the text and write the questions in the correct spaces.

Are you looking for something different?

Come to *Burning Man*

Come and experience art and survival in the desert for one week.

August 29th – September 5th
Tickets $250

a How do you get there?

b What is Burning Man?

c Why is it called 'Burning Man'?

d What is there to do at Burning Man?

e What's the weather like?

f What does the place look like?

g What happens when Burning Man is over?

h What should I bring?

Every year for one week about 25,000 people go to the Nevada desert from around the world to an event which is called Burning Man. A 'city' is built in the middle of the Black Rock Desert. They call this city Black Rock City. They spend the week living together in the city and making art while they are there.

Before you think about going to Burning Man, read these Frequently Asked Questions (FAQs) to get an idea of what Burning Man is. It could be just right for you.

FAQs

Q. 1 ....

A. Burning Man is an experiment in living with other people. If you want to really understand Burning Man, you have to try it.

Q. 2 ....

A. You can drive to the Black Rock Desert in your car and camp, or you can come in a camper van. Many people come in an art car decorated especially for the occasion, like this one.

Q. 3 ....

A. Black Rock City is organised as two thirds (2/3) of a circle. 'The Man' is put in the centre.

Q. 4 ....

A. Water, food and shelter (a tent or other place to sleep) are the things that you must bring with you so that you can survive. Everything else you bring is up to you. Many people bring toys or costumes to play and to make art.

Q.5 ....
A. The weather in late August/early September is usually warm, but it can be really cold. People at Burning Man have had many evenings below 40°F (4°C) and daytime temperatures over 100°F (38°C).

Q.6 ....
A. The first thing to do is participate. You are not there to watch, you are there to make art and live in a community. Nobody at Burning Man is a spectator; you're there to build your own new world. Use your imagination.
And … you're there to survive. You have to drink water all the time and you have to cover yourself in sunblock because the sun is very strong. Remember, you cannot buy anything at Black Rock City except coffee and ice.

Q.7 ....
A. The Man is a huge 75 ft (20m) high piece of art. It is at the centre of the city and it is the heart of this event. On Saturday night, at the end of a week, the Man is burnt.

Q.8 ....
A. You leave as you came. When you go from Burning Man, you leave no trace. Everything you built, you take apart and take it with you. The rubbish that you made leaves with you and the Black Rock Desert returns to its perfect condition. There are volunteers who stay for weeks to clean up the desert.
But you take the world you built with you. When you have experienced Burning Man your world will change – forever.

2 **Write answers to the following questions.**

a What is Black Rock City? ....

b What is the best way to understand Burning Man?
....

c What is an art car? ....

d What is organised to look like part of a circle?
....

e What are the things that you must bring to the event?
....

f What are the maximum and minimum temperatures?
....

g Who can participate in the event? ....

h What can you buy at Burning Man? ....
....

i What is 'the Man'? ....

j What happens after the event is over? ....
....

3 **Use these words and phrases from the text to complete the sentences.**

| at the heart of | camper van | experiment | it's up to you |
| participate | shelter | spectators | sunblock | survive | trace |

a My parents are going to travel through Europe in their new .... , so they won't need to stay in hotels.

b Scientists and researchers often do an .... to find out some new information.

c It was raining and very cold so we needed .... for the night – a place to stay.

d Would you like to .... in the competition? If you win, the prize is a trip to New York.

e Where do you want to go for dinner? It's your birthday so .... You can make the decision.

f When we arrived at the stadium there were 50,000 .... waiting for the match to begin.

g I looked for my dog everywhere, but there was no .... of her anywhere. Not a thing.

h It's impossible for people to .... on the moon, because there is no oxygen.

i If you sit on the beach you must wear .... , so that your skin is not hurt.

j The prize-giving ceremony is .... the annual film festival.

●●B Writing: Making your story interesting

1 Read these two ways of telling the same story. Text A is a complete story and Text B is the beginning of the same story.

A

One day, Robert Barnes was in his garden and he was planting flowers. He heard a voice behind him. The voice said "Leave us alone". He turned around. There was no one there. He looked into the history of the house and found that the house had a long history. Many bad things happened there.

B

One beautiful, sunny day last week, I was at home, just relaxing in my garden. I knew that spring was on its way, and I felt like planting some flowers. I started digging the hole. It was hot work, but I felt happy and optimistic. Suddenly, even though I was hot, and the sun was burning down on my back, I felt the air around me go cold. The hairs on my arms stood up. It grew extremely quiet. Even the birds seemed to have stopped singing. I stood there, spade in hand, knowing, with a feeling of dread, that I was not alone …

2 What are the differences between the two ways of telling the story? Complete the table.

	A	B
Who tells the story?		
How does the writer describe the scene?		
How are feelings described?		
Does the writer use a lot of detail?		

3 Read Text B again and find words to write in the table.

Words and expressions to describe feelings	Adjectives and expressions to describe things

4 Now read Text A again. How many words and expressions can you find to describe feelings and things?

> The words you choose can make your writing more interesting. Many words have similar meanings, but some words add more to the description than others.

5 Find the best word to describe these situations.

a I .... to get away from the ghost.

   1 raced   2 ran fast

b Imagine my .... when it began to overtake me.

   1 nervousness   2 terror

c I .... for help.

   1 called   2 screamed

d But there was only a .... silence.

   1 complete   2 deathly

6 Adverbs can make your writing more interesting, too. Find suitable places after the verbs in blue in Text B, to add the following adverbs.

> energetically
> freezing
> straight
> silently
> warmly
> completely

Now continue the story in Text B. Look at the picture. Circle the best words and expressions to make the story more interesting.

I don't know how long I must have stood like that, (a) *frozen in terror / straight / thinking*. Then I heard a (b) *loud / gentle / terrifying* voice whisper my name. I turned around (c) *at once / quickly / slowly*. There, in my garden, stood the most (d) *horrible / beautiful / familiar* woman, holding a (e) *young / big / noisy* baby in her arms. Her dress was (f) *new / trendy / old-fashioned*, as if from the 1920s. Her hair hung (g) *loosely / tied / pulled back* down her back. But her eyes …. When I looked into her eyes, I felt myself turning into (h) *water / ice / her*. Her (i) *blue / twinkling / blank* eyes (j) *looked / glanced / stared* into mine. But I knew she wasn't looking at me. She was looking (k) *past / up and down at / through* me. She wasn't (l) *alive / friendly / a stranger*. I was looking at a (m) *person / mother / ghost*.

Answer key

Unit 1
Reading
1 a 3 b 1 c 4 d 2
2 a French/English b Jerry c Jessy d Cape Town
   e the part of Wyoming where Jerry is staying
   f Sydney g Tricia's
3 a T (Tricia: 'the beaches are great')
   b F (Jerry: 'it's in the middle of nowhere')
   c T (Jerry: 'I like cities better than the country!')
   d F (Jessy: 'The Great Barrier Reef is huge – more than 2000 kilometres long!')
   e T (Mum: 'We also took a boat ride on the Saint Lawrence River.')
   f F ('Cape Town is at the foot of Table Mountain'.)
4 a interesting (3) b modern (3) c different (1)
   d huge (1) e better (4)
5 a 4 b 2 c 3 d 5 e 1 f 6
6 a can't wait b nightlife c in the middle of nowhere
   d my idea of fun   e watch the world go by
   f at the foot

Writing
1 Grand Canyon, USA
2 b, c, f
3 a The sender's address is not used in postcards, and dates are not normally used in postcards.
   b Formal openings, Dear … are not normally used in postcards
   c 'I wish you were here!'
   d This is a common phrase in postcards.
4 *Example answer*
   The Taj Mahal is fantastic! It's a beautiful building in Agra, India. It was built by Shah Jahan in 1631, when his second wife died. It's made entirely of marble and jewels brought from all over India. It took 22 years to complete, by 20,000 workers, and 1,000 elephants! Wish you were here!
   (your name)

Unit 2
Reading
1 a He is having a bad dream.
   b She is feeling nervous.
   c He is feeling angry.
   d She often forgets things.
   e He is feeling hot and sweating a lot.
   f She has a headache.
2 Meaning 1

3 a T b T c T d F ('Don't drink any caffeine.')
   e F ('Do exercise every day.')
5 a What is stress?
   b Different kinds of stress
   c How to deal with stress
6 a when you don't know what to do because there are too many things in your life
   b things that cause stress
   c change
   d good: if it's a challenge, like a race ... bad: if you're leaving friends
   e exercise, laughter, talking about your problems
   f sugar, snacks, caffeine, chocolate, cakes

Writing
1 a because there are many words he doesn't know.
   b so she gets stressed.
   c but she worries about her pronunciation.
   d but he doesn't know how.
2 a but b so c because d but e because f but
3 *Example answers*
   Why is learning English a good idea?
   Because it can help you get a better job, because it is the most widely spoken international language, because it's nice to be able to understand films and songs in English.
   Things about English that can be stressful:
   Pronunciation and grammar, and learning new words.
   Things you can do to help yourself:
   You can take a deep breath so that you relax.
   You can keep a notebook so that you can write down things.
   You can keep repeating things so that you can remember them.

Unit 3
Reading
1 Theme a is the answer. Kirsty's story (b) is used to illustrate the influence of the media; popular magazines (c) are mentioned in the article but it is not the most important idea.
2 a She wants to read about famous models.
   b They have a lot of information and have nice pictures.
   c She doesn't have a healthy diet and she exercises more than normal.
   d She worries that Kirsty is developing an eating disorder.
   e She thinks that they are responsible for her daughter's situation.

f It's OK to have ambitions, but not OK to think about them all the time.

3 a role models b pocket money c obsession
d ambition e influence f eating disorder
g responsible

4 a eating disorder
b pocket money
c obsession
d responsible
e role models
f ambition
g influence

Writing

1 a 240. (This is the sample.)
b between the ages of 18 and 35 (This is called the age group.)
c 70% (or 168)
d sitcoms
e yes, just a few (7% of the sample)

2, 3
a F (only 3 out of 10 like sitcoms)
b T
c T
d F (5 like documentaries, 7 like the news)
e F (3 hours a day)
f F (8 people like soap operas)

4 a More b A lot c most d average e Not many

5 Question 2 (Preferences)

6 *Example answer*
65% of people read a magazine more than once a week.
25% of people read a magazine once a week.
6% of people read it less than once a week.
4% of people don't read a magazine at all.

Unit 4

Reading

1 a Steve Irwin
b Terri, a lion tamer
c Queensland, Australia
d snakes

2 a a reptile expert
b he moves them to safe environments
c she was a lion tamer
d as a child his hobby was to collect reptiles
e to milk their venom
f people can learn about the animals and learn to respect them
g because they're scared of them
h when he got his first snake, at the age of six
i after their popular TV series, 'The Crocodile Hunter'
j with his bare hands

3 a 4 b 8 c 5 d 7 e 6 f 2 g 3 h 1

4 a dangerous b respect c exciting d unusual
e popular f bare g reptiles h tourist i lion
j environment

Writing

1 **Advertisement a:** Carrie is looking for a job.
Advertisement b: Kimber and Kimber Associates is offering a job.

2 **Ad a**
a 4, Carrie
b 2, English and computer skills
c 5, 3759670
d 3, no experience, but a fast learner
e 1, temporary office work
Ad b
a 5, Kimber and Kimber Associates
b 1, temporary staff
c 3, a good salary, free sports club, free lunches
d 2, good presentation, English and computing skills
e 4, 75953795

4 *Example answer*
needs an assistant
Hours would suit a student (part-time, three hours a day)
Requirements: hard-working, organised person, good English, some computer experience
We offer: a good salary, experience in publishing, and free copies of our magazines
Call Sam, on 07785458924

Unit 5

Reading

1 The text is probably not (a) because although there is love here perhaps, there are also people watching, he is 'in danger' and there are 3 men waiting outside. The text could, perhaps, be a science fiction story (b) but this is unlikely unless everyone is an alien! The text is probably from a thriller/spy story (c) because of all the people watching, the ordinary station setting etc. Of course, it could be a horror story (d) but there is no evidence for this, so it probably isn't.

2 The mistakes in the picture are:
– Amelie's hair is short (the text says 'with her long black hair')
– there are 4 men standing outside (the text says 'there were 3 men standing outside.') – one woman at the coffee stall has a red hat (the text says 'two young women in yellow hard hats')

3 a 2 b 3 c 1 d 3 e 3

4 a scanned b escalator c roof d normal
e worry about f stared g looked away h incredible

5 a stared b escalator c incredible d normal
e looked away f worry about g roof h scanned

Writing

1 a 3 b 4 c 6 d 2 e 5 f 1 g 7 h 8
2 *Example answer*
   Take the second right. Go along (to the end of the street), and take the first left. Turn left, and it's on the right.
3 B
4 **Map A**
   When you get to the station, go straight ahead and go to the corner of that street. The street then turns left, and left again. Go along and take the third right. We're on the right, opposite the park.
5 *Example answer*
   When you get to the station, turn right and go along to the corner. The street turns left at the corner. Go along, and pass / don't take the first right. We're just after that, on the right, opposite the park.

Unit 6

Reading

1 a Our brains throw away information we don't need to keep.
   b episodic memory
   c semantic memory keeps information that you will need in a test
   d procedural memory stores procedures
2 a T b T c F d F e T f T g F
3 Short-term memory: (part of the brain that) keeps information we don't need to remember for a long time.
   Long-term memory: (part of the brain that) keeps things we need to remember for a long time.
   Episodic memory: (part of the brain that) keeps things that happened in your life.
   Procedural memory: (part of the brain that) keeps the way you do things/procedures.
   Semantic memory: (part of the brain that) keeps facts and dates.
4 a filing cabinet
   b wrong
   c episode
   d memory
   e memories
   f store
   g remember

Writing

1 They want to make contact with their old friends Bear, Rhino and Fox to get the band together again.
2 a, c, d, e, f
3 *Example answer*
   Remember me? I'm Ricardo Bruni (aka Bear)!
   I was at The International School in Los Angeles too, and we played in the band, The Zoo. I played the guitar and the piano. Do you know I became a music teacher? After school, I went to New York. My first job was teaching kids to play the guitar.

It was OK, but the money was terrible! Then I went back to Italy and started working as a music teacher at a school. There I met Anna, and she's now my wife! We got married last year. Now we've got a baby, Marco.
4 *Example answer*
   Hi, I'm Jiao Tsim (aka Fox)! I was at The International School in Los Angeles too, and we played in the band, The Zoo. I was the singer. After school, I went back to China. I studied English at Beijing University. Last year I wrote a book of children's stories. Now I'm working on another book. I'm not married yet – I'm too busy!

Unit 7

Reading

1 a the fourth ad/the ad for pottery
   b the third ad/the ad for website design
   c the first ad/the ad for Capoeira
   d the last ad/the ad for Limelight Workshops
   e the first ad/the ad for Capoeira
2 a the activities in the second ad/website design
   b the Limelight Workshops
   c capoeira
   d a website
   e photography
   f capoeira
   g capoeira
   h pottery
   i photography
3 a creativity b perfect c region d share
   e like-minded f slaves g confident h baked
4 a slaves
   b perfect
   c like-minded
   d baked
   e creativity
   f share
   g confident

Writing

1 a music workshops
   b Duxton Hall
   c Saturdays 9–12.30
   d you can phone or look at the website
   e 'Come and make music!' 'You know you want to!'
2 a and b are NOT included
3 a, b, c, d
4 *Example answer*
   Do you like the outdoors, and walking?
   Come and join our hiking club!
   We'll meet every Saturday at 9 am, returning from our hike by 5 pm.
   You only have to pay your travel costs to and from the area we visit, and your lunch!
   For more information, go to our website: www.kings.ac.uk/hiking

Unit 8
Reading

1 Though alternatives a, b and d are all possible, c is the best because it most closely relates to the topic of the article – the chemistry of fear.
2 a big waves b Yes, he does.
  c what they do about their fear
  d adrenalin e new and exciting situations
3 a He
  b He
4 a 2 b 2 c 1 d 2 e 2
5 a frightened
  b anger
  c dangerous
  d friendly
  e confident
  f bored

Writing

1 a The writer doesn't understand people because they don't say what they mean. The main idea is at the beginning.
  b in the first two sentences of the paragraph
  c sentences 3–7.
2 The correct order is 3, 1, 4, 2, 5, 6 or (2 1 3 5 4 6)
3 The correct order is a, c, g, f, e, j, h, i, b, d
4 d

Unit 9
Reading

2 a 1 b 3 c 2
3 a 'Precious moments' on Clarence Road
  b get a personal tutor or go to a computer class
  c websites for second hand equipment
  d can't use the new software well
  e the online tutorial with the class to demonstrate the procedure.
4 a the videos in the collection
  b second hand record players
  c program
  d your best videos
  e my father
  f record players
5 a repair b second hand c collection d valuable
  e install f old fashioned g properly h managed
6 a valuable
  b properly
  c install
  d collection
  e second hand
  f old-fashioned
  g managed
  h repair

Writing

1 The nouns have been repeated instead of being replaced by pronouns, the second time they are mentioned.
2 a it b it c they d them
3 a
  A lot of people hate answering machines but I love them. I've got one at home and as soon as I get home I turn it on and listen to the messages on it. It is also useful because I can hear who is calling and only answer if I want to.
  b
  Mariella can't live without her hairdryer. She uses it every day because she thinks her looks are very important. She even took it when we went camping but the batteries were flat and of course she couldn't plug it in anywhere.
4 a technology
  b everyone's
  c designers
  d the wearable PC
  e The MP3 jacket / wearable PC
  f the jacket's
  g the reader's / the boss of the person who is reading this
  h the boss
  i the colleagues
  j the colleagues
5 (Not all the sentences change. You only need to use pronouns when a noun is repeated.)
  a ---
  b I really want one of them.
  c With them, it's possible to make videos.
  d ----
  e ----
  f Within seconds, he or she can see the same thing as you have just seen!
  g ---
  h It gets better all the time.
  i -----
  j I suppose I'll want it / that then, too.

Unit 10
Reading

1 a Argentina b Poland c Singapore
2 Joanna is in Poland, Anthony is in Argentina and Naomi is in Singapore.
3 a Mrs S, the head teacher
  b Naomi and Terry's guests
  c The Argentinean farmer
  d Naomi
  e Joanna
  f Anthony
  g Naomi and Terry
  h Joanna
  i Cath

4 a I did something wrong.
  b Take last night, for example.
  c I'm really looking forward to it.
  d absolutely fantastic
  e there was something wrong
  f they didn't mind
  g come out
  h key-ring

Writing

1 a 4 b 1 c 2 d 3
2 Message c is the only formal message.
3 a 3 b 4 c 1 d 2
4 a 2 b 1 c 2 d 2 e 2
5 a Informal, ('hi' is informal, and so is 'About 8?' instead of a full sentence)
  b informal (it's a text message)
  c formal ('Dear', 'Best wishes', friendly but not 'familiar' language)
6 *Example answers*
  a I'd love to, thanks. See you then.
  b sorry, working 2moro
  c Dear Sarah, Thank you very much for your kind invitation. I'm sorry I won't be able to come, though, as I will be away in Japan next week.
    Best wishes
    Matthew

Unit 11

Reading

1 Name: Caroline Rippin
  Age: 30
  Occupation: actor or actress
  Where she does it: in the theatre, in schools (a bit of TV)
  Favourite music: jazz, blues, soul
  Favourite smell: watermelon
2 a her parents
  b they rehearse
  c she directs a schools' theatre group and makes shows with the children
  d Caroline did. She went to drama school later.
  e actors say it is when they are at drama school
  f Caroline does
  g a teacher at her school
  h an actor – because he forgot his lines
3 a 6 b 7 c 4 d 3 e 1 f 10 g 8 h 2 i 5 j 9
4 *Example answers*
  a What is it like at drama school?
  b How did you become interested in studying drama?
  c What kind of acting do you do?
  d How do you find learning lines?
  e Have you ever forgotten your lines? / Is it difficult to remember your lines?
  f What do you do to keep up your acting skills?
  g How do you like to relax?
  h What is your favourite smell?

Writing

1 a 5 b 9 c 4 d 7 e 2 f 3 g 1 h 6 i 8
2 Example interview
  How old are you?
  I'll be 25 in a week's time!
  Where did you grow up?
  In a small town in south west Scotland.
  What memories do you have of your childhood?
  I remember riding bikes in the woods, building tree houses, swimming in the lakes …
  Where did you go to university?
  I went to university in Edinburgh. I did English and Spanish.
  What was your first job?
  Teaching English in Peru, three years ago.
  What were the best things about Peru?
  The Peruvian people, the food, the mountains – and the music.
  What was your most memorable experience in Peru?
  Climbing up Machu Pichu at sunrise – magical.
  What are your future plans?
  I want to travel to other countries, like China, Japan, India – but eventually I hope to settle back in Scotland, and start a language school there.

Unit 12

Reading

1 1 Ian Wilmut 2 Julia "Butterfly" Hill
  3 Craig Newmark 4 Jamie Oliver
  5 Wangari Maathai
2 a movement
  b laboratory
  c environment
  d mammals
  e biologists
  f inspire
3 a a cloned sheep
  b the tree that Julia stayed in
  c an online bulletin board
  d Jamie Oliver's cooking school
  e Wangari Maathai
  f Julia "Butterfly" Hill and Wangari Maathai
4 a protect
  b chef
  c clone
  d destroy
  e bulletin board
  f cells
  g human rights
  h unemployed

Writing

1 a Bernie b Catherine
2 For: I am writing to give my support, I want to become a member.
  Against: I do not agree with your ideas, Your organisation is very dangerous.

3 *Example answer*

I am writing to express my opinion that animal research is wrong. Animals need us to protect them, as they are unable to protect themselves. They have feelings, and, just like humans, they can feel pain. Therefore it is against their rights to be used for cosmetic testing. Please think about what you are doing to animals.

I am writing to give my support to your organization. Although I love animals, they are NOT as important as humans, and they do not have the same rights. We depend on animals for clothing and food, and if we do not use them for medical research, how would be know that medicines were safe to use, or could save human lives? Thank you for the good work you are doing.

Unit 13

Reading

1 *Suggested Answers:*

David Beckham – kinesthetic, Albert Einstein – logical-mathematical,

William Shakespeare – linguistic, Jane Goodall – naturalistic,

Oprah Winfrey – interpersonal, Anne Frank – intrapersonal,

Martin Luther King – existential, Ludwig van Beethoven – musical,

Frank Lloyd Wright – spatial

2 a linguistic b logical c mathematical d spatial
e kinesthetic f musical g personal h existential
i naturalistic (natural)

Writing

1 Paragraph 1: Personality
Paragraph 2: Interests and actifvities
Paragraph 3: Travel

2 a F b T c T d T e F

3 a 3 b 1 c 2

Possible answers

– languages because she likes to travel
– music because she is musical
– geography because she's interested in other places
– anthropology because she's interested in other cultures

4 *Suggested answer*

I think I am a quiet, serious person, and a good listener. But I also have a sense of humour!
I enjoy photography, and writing, especially poetry. I wrote a book of poems which was published last year. I also love music, and I play the violin in an orchestra. My other hobbies are mountain climbing, hiking and sailing.
In the future, I hope to travel more, especially to Africa to do wildlife photography.

Unit 14

Reading

1 Name: Zaha Hadid
Country of origin: Iraq
Occupation: architect
Type of character: Lively? A bit crazy? Sometimes angry? Friendly? Energetic, etc.

2 a sports stadium b diva c bad-tempered d cares
e designing f contemporary g rolls her eyes
h gigantic i intellect j passionate

3 a rolled her eyes
b passionate
c gigantic
d intelligence
e bad-tempered
f designed
g stadium
h cares
i contemporary
j diva

4 *Example answers*

a She's a woman, she grew up in Iraq, she's not a quiet person.

b in London

c She's a big woman, very intelligent and with a huge personality.

d She gets very excited about architecture.

e She won a competition to design an opera house in Cardiff, but the public decided they wanted a stadium instead, so the opera house was never built.

Writing

1 b

2, 3
beautiful, P tall, P white, P peaceful, P friendly,
P exciting, P dramatic, P gigantic, P ugliest, N wide,
N fat N

4 a
paragraph a: It is two hundred and fifty years old;
paragraph b: It was built in 2004;
paragraph c: It is only a few years old.
b
paragraph a: It is tall and white. It looks very peaceful and it is friendly;
paragraph b: It is tall and dramatic. It looks like a gigantic vegetable;
paragraph c: It is wide and rather fat. It looks like a tomato.
c
paragraph a: Every time I go there I feel happy;
paragraph b: some people call it the gherkin;
paragraph c: It's next to some beautiful old buildings, so it doesn't look right.
d
paragraph a It's one of the most beautiful buildings in London.

paragraph b It's one of the most exciting sights in London.

paragraph c It's one of the ugliest buildings in London.

5 *Example answers*

It was built in 2004.

It's in Edinburgh.

The roof looks like an upside down boat. Some people think it looks as if it was built by a child, out of Lego. Many think it is the ugliest building in Britain.

I think it is very modern and European-looking.

It was designed by Spanish architect Enric Mirales, and won an architecture award.

6 *Example answers*

One of the most exciting buildings in Edinburgh is the new Scottish Parliament. It is only a few years old. It was built in 2004, designed by Spanish architect Enric Mirales. It looks like a gigantic upside down boat. The windows are particularly interesting. I think it is an example of one of Britain's most modern and forward-thinking buildings.

OR

One of the ugliest buildings in Edinburgh is the new Scottish Parliament. It is only a few years old. It was built in 2004, designed by Spanish architect Enric Mirales. It is difficult to believe it won an award for its design – it looks like a gigantic superstore, swimming pool and car park all put together by a child using Lego bricks. The windows in particular, are decorated with very ugly designs that look like hairdryers.

Unit 15

Reading

1 Things that stop us from sleeping

noise

sitting in a chair

temperature

altitude

Why?

Loud noises stop us from sleeping.

We need to be horizontal when we sleep.

It's hard to sleep if you are too hot or too cold.

Above 4,000m you need to breathe differently.

2 a 1 b 3 c 2 d 3 e 3

3 a oxygen b horizontal c depression d notice
e treatment f caffeine g altitude

4 a oxygen b treatment c horizontal d depression
e altitude f caffeine g notice

Writing

2 diet and rest: a, b, f, i
home life: g, h
money: e, h, j
social life: c, d, g

3 Marco's order (suggested answer):
enough sleep 1
good food 1

hobbies 7
friends 5
plenty of money 10
regular medical check-ups 3
people who care about you 5
a nice place to live 8
regular exercise 4
interesting work 8

4 Paragraph 1 Diet and fitness
Paragraph 2 Social life
Paragraph 3 Home life
Paragraph 4 Money

5 Paragraph 1: That doesn't mean …
Paragraph 2: And if you are new …
Paragraph 3: It's nice …
Paragraph 4: I know a lot of rich people …

6 *Suggested answers:*
b (opening) a (closing)

7 If you want to stay healthy …
… if you have good friends and people who care for you …
Where you live and where you work …
…. having a lot of money …

Unit 16

Reading

1 a 2 b 1 c 7 d 6 e 5 f 3 g 8 h 4

2 a the name of the city that is built in the desert during Burning Man
b to try it
c a specially decorated car
d Black Rock City
e water, food, and shelter
f over 100°F (38°C) and below 40°F (4°C)
g everyone
h ice and coffee
i a 75 ft (20 m) piece of art
j you take everything with you and the Black Rock Desert returns to normal

3 a camper van b experiment c shelter
d participate e it's up to you f spectators g trace
h survive i sunblock j at the heart of

Writing

2 *Suggested answers*
Who tells the story?
A Third person, someone who is not Robert Barnes.
B First person, the person who the story happened to, Robert Barnes.
How does the writer describe the scene?
A He was in the garden and he was planting flowers. (the writer does not give much information)
B It was a beautiful day and I decided to plant some flowers.

How are feelings described?

A They are not described.

B I felt the air go cold and the hairs on my arms stood up. Suddenly I had the feeling that I was not alone.

Does the writer use a lot of detail?

A No, there is not much detail.

B This version has more detail.

3 Words and expressions to describe feelings

happy and optimistic

the hairs on my arms stood up

with a feeling of dread

Adjectives and expressions to describe things

beautiful, sunny (day)

hot (work)

cold (air)

burning (sun)

extremely quiet

4 only one: bad (things)

5 **a** 1 **b** 2 **c** 2 **d** 2

6 digging energetically

burning warmly

go silently

stood up straight

stopped singing completely

stood there freezing

Suggested answers

a frozen in terror

b gentle

c slowly / at once / quickly

d beautiful

e young

f old-fashioned

g loosely

h ice

i blank

j stared

k through

l alive

m ghost